I0429815

# CHANGING AMERICAN CULTURE

ISBN-13: 978-1502331779
ISBN-10: 1502331772

# Changing American Culture

## TABLE OF CONTENTS

# PREFACE

Every day we wake to the news of stories that indicate the problems that have been obstacles to the advancement of people and society from a century ago continue to persist and deteriorate with no end in sight beyond the precipices. We rarely hear of any solutions but instead see our elected officials constantly embroiled in partisan bickering due to ideologs positioning themselves for re-election. The consequence of legislative gridlock coupled with an apathetic citizenry reinforced by the lack of future vision is further erosion of the health of society as a whole.

This book attempts to tackle some of the major issues of our times in the hope people among voters and public leaders may begin to change their focus from personality and ideological conflict to conciliation, compromise and constructive action through a more efficient spending of public funds. Too often government has focused on punishing the citizenry instead of enabling them to fulfill their need for the pursuit of lawful happiness as guaranteed by the Constitution of the United States of America.

# CHAPTER ONE - OUR EDUCATIONAL SYSTEM

American children are usually performing at the lower tiers of academic excellence when compared to other developed nations. The educational stew has been stirred and stirred, new ingredients tried, and the political temperature cranked up several notches. SAT scores are slowly inching up for the past 5 years; however, this may reflect changes in the test that help to improve scores, or greater numbers of students resorted to SAT preparatory courses, or teachers helping students to become better test takers.

Regardless of what public education has become, it certainly is not anticipating the profound changes that is rapidly taking place in society due to technology. Computers are not properly utilized in the classrooms, and emphasizing repetition, memorization, and test taking performance will not turn out the type of people who will be able to think, make appropriate decisions, be employable, or even survive in the next 20 years. Students graduating from college enter the work world with knowledge that will be useless, either because technology will make their educations irrelevant, or their technical expertise will be more employable for one-tenth the salary in a foreign country.

Following are observations, comments, and suggestions for overhauling our nation's public education curriculum and system. We need to get more "bang" and less "gangs" for the buck. We need to build a thirst for knowledge, a desire for pursuing success, rather than using an obsolete measuring stick to create nine failures for every success. We need to put more individual choice in schools, so students can feel empowered to learn what they feel is most relevant and useful in their lives, and not be forced to move with the herd, either too slowly for some, or too fast for others. It's no wonder so many students are bored with school, or hate it.

| Old School | New Pedagogy |
| --- | --- |

A. Purpose

| | Old School | New Pedagogy |
| --- | --- | --- |
| 1. | Educational purpose | Politics and money issues |
| 2. | Elective coursework | Basic 3 R's, few electives |
| 3. | After school programs | Few school programs |
| 4. | School clubs | Few school activities |
| 5. | Organized sports | Few school teams |
| 6. | Physical education | Few school classes |
| 7. | Emphasis on learning | Emphasis on testing |
| 8. | Sensible curriculum | More useless subjects |
| 9. | Moral lessons | Short on moral values |
| 10. | Positive results | Low retention & test scores |

B.  Attitudes

| | | |
|---|---|---|
| 1. | Respect teachers | Disrespect teachers |
| 2. | Get along with classmates | Dislike and hate classmates |
| 3. | Listen intently | Daydream, talk, not listening |
| 4. | Follow instructions | Disregard instructions |
| 5. | Ask permission | Blurt out, interrupt teachers |
| 6. | Quiet while studying | Talk to friends, not studying |
| 7. | Personal responsibility | Complain work is too hard |

C.  Techniques

| | | |
|---|---|---|
| 1. | Classroom discipline | Reacting to behaviors |
| 2. | Punishing disruptions | Time outs and pleads |
| 3. | Detention for misbehavior | Few after school detention |
| 4. | Parental participation | Parents blame teachers |
| 5. | Parental supervision | Parents blame teachers |
| 6. | Religious release time | Sectarianism |
| 7. | Integrated approach | Special education privileges |
| 8. | Multi-tiered learning pace | Herding and standardized |
| 9. | Positive modeling | Graduated step learning |
| 10. | Hands on learning | Limited hands on study |
| 11. | Inspiration & motivation | Boring material taught |
| 12. | Expertise & excellence | Shallow knowledge |
| 13. | Achievements rewarded | Few reward programs |
| 14. | Learning based grades | Test taking ability grades |
| 15. | Relevant homework | Busy work |
| 16. | Simplicity & honesty | Complex and confusing |
| 17. | Straight forward approach | Confusing and contradictory |

D.	Support

| 1. | Patriotism- flag salute | No flag salute or pledge |
| 2. | Community pride | Pride? Who cares? |
| 3. | School safety | Everyone are "at risk" |
| 4. | Suspension not a reward | Students act out to get freed |
| 5. | Expulsion not rewarding | Students enjoy ditching |
| 6. | Support for education | Political positioning pretense |
| 7. | Legal support of teachers | Teacher's have few rights |

E.	Teacher Qualifications and Mindset

| 1. | Commitment to educating | Pay and benefits motivated |
| 2. | Exciting and rewarding | Time off with good benefits |
| 3. | Neat and professional | Blue jeans and casual |
| 4. | Honest, fair, impartial | Lives imitate TV sitcoms |
| 5. | Serious, mature, helpful | Disinterested, stressed out |
| 6. | Engaging, inspiring | Disinterested and boring |
| 7. | Dedicated and informed | Reliant on teachers' editions |
| 8. | Thorough knowledge | Unsure of large data base |
| 9. | Salaries on par w/trades | Wide variation standards |
| 10. | Meticulous and courteous | Sloppy and rude |
| 11. | On time and punctuality | Last minute arrivals/excuses |
| 12. | Trustworthy and honesty | Situational deception & lies |
| 13. | Committed with pride | Whatever is convenient |
| 14. | Honorable & considerate | Self-centered/inconsiderate |

F.    Why can't Johnny...?

1.    Read and comprehend complex material
2.    Correctly complete math operations and applications
3.    Write sensibly, legibly, and concisely
4.    Think creatively, rationally, and positively
5.    Analyze patterns, abstractions, and associations
6.    Make logical and good decisions based on situations
7.    Act appropriately and respectfully
8.    Speak intelligently; articulate and communicate
9.    Remember, recall, repeat, and summarize
10.   Compare and contrast data and from examples
11.   Listen and follow instructions and directions
12.   Desire to learn; satisfy a sense of curiosity
13.   Ask well-formulated questions
14.   Consider plausible options and alternatives
15.   Get along with others
16.   Respect authority figures
17.   Be trustworthy and dependable
18.   Accept personal responsibility for results
19.   Obey school and classroom rules
20.   Desire to succeed and strive for potential

G. Contradictions between values taught in school versus the actual social realities

| Success values taught in school | Real world values |
|---|---|
| 1. Education gets good jobs | Connections for best jobs |
| 2. Listen & follow directions | Creativity and popularity |
| 3. Authority sets standards | Personal standards |
| 4. Compare and validate | Do your own thing |
| 5. Conform to the norms | Go your own way and path |
| 6. Excel in testing | Work smarter, not harder |
| 7. Don't socialize in class | Popularity equals success |
| 8. Don't talk while learning | Multi-task, adjust to noise |
| 9. Be serious-don't joke | Levity helps group dynamics |
| 10. Don't be a class clown | Humor is a rewarding |

H. Urgently Needed Educational Reforms
1. Class size
- Ratio of 1:15 for avg. students; 1:10 for gifted; 1:5 for special needs students, and less than 45 in lecture halls
- Team teaching & combining classrooms for lectures
2. Classroom management
- Cameras, recording video, audio controlled and monitored
- Disruptors immediately escorted to detention hall
- ·Routine and persistent disruptors get behavior management
- specialist/psych intervention and cleared before readmission
3. Computer applications
- Ideal of one terminal per one to two 2 students

- Lesson modules at individualized pace beyond minimal schedule
- Networking with area schools for group learning

4. Visual aids
- More effective use of video and CD educational program
- On-line educational materials to supplement lecture and texts
- Computer media instead of paper

5. Tiered learning groups
- Eager, fast, and/or gifted learners
- Average paced learners
- Slow learners/non-behavioral causation
- Behavioral dysfunction and incarcerated
- Special education

6. Diagnostic assessment
- Aptitude and interest inventories at appropriate grade levels
- Memory, analytical ability, reasoning skills, creativity,
- Learning style, attention and focus propensities, etc.

7. Student misbehaviors
- Attention seeking & inappropriate speech or actions
- Verbal correction, counseling, write essay, apologize to class
- Moderately disruptive language and behaviors:
- 1st incident = warning; 2nd = detention; 3rd = parent confer
- Highly dramatic and disruptive language and behaviors
- 1st incident = detention, parent conference; 2nd = suspension
- Violence, attempted violence, or threats to commit violence:

- Toward Self = detention, psych intervention, and parent conference
- To others = detention, suspension or expulsion up to including
- Administrative investigation, referral to law enforcement action

8. Protecting teachers
- No law enforcement involvement until after administrative investigation by school district investigators (no witch hunts)
- Referral to law enforcement investigation if not cleared
- Attorneys for teachers present during teacher interrogations
- Reinstatement of humane punishment at grades below
- Teacher self defense permitted if attacked

9. Curriculum reforms
- Must be relevant and not just memorizing
- Practical education
- Foundational skills in reading, writing and mathematics
- Preparation for living and working in a technological world
- Social morals that enhance civility and societal stability

10. Cultural enrichment
- International relations, cooperation, and conflict resolution
- Patriotism, legal system, politics, parenting, and humanism
- Effects of globalization, regionalism and centralism
- Religious, cultural, and historical perspectives

11. Economics and finance
- Domestic and world banking system
- Interstate and international trade
- Real estate, stocks, bonds and other legitimate investments

- Honesty in marketing and advertising
12. Science
   - General physics, chemistry, biology, anatomy, and astronomy
   - Pharmacology
   - Immunology
   - Genetics and human genomics
   - Microbiology
   - Energy & alternative energies
   - Environmental sciences
13. Technology
   - Computer miniaturization & applications
   - Engineering (all areas)
   - Architecture and building materials innovation
14. Social and political
   - Treating and healing dysfunctional personalities
   - Opinion research and political policies
   - Constructive decision-making techniques and strategies
   - Humanistic development and evolution
15. Standardization
   - Testing
   - Grading
16. Individualization
   - Pace of learning
   - Personal interest elective courses
   - Decision-making strategies
   - Depoliticize educational reforms
   - Politicians may not pass laws without prior studies review

- Panels of educators to discuss and justifying changes
- Funding formulas not subject to partisan political pandering
- Teachers not primarily blamed for lower student scores; test
- Scores are computer assessed to compensate for individual student progress history etc.

The future of education will be revolutionary. Students will discover that the correlation between future employment benefits and level of educational attainment will be illusory, and in most cases, a big fat lie. Technology will enhance the learning curve of those willing and thirsty to learn, and assist the rest to become more efficient learners. Manipulation of data, analysis, forecasting, and data retention will be the domain of nano-computers worn on students' wrists. Students will ask their computer companions questions, or give the parameters of problems, and the master computer will supply the appropriate answers, solutions, options, and choices to the student via their wristwatch computer companion.

The basic 3R's will still need to be taught, and basic overviews given in all fundamental curriculum subjects. However, once students have learned the basic relationships and concepts, their computer companion will fill in the gaps, the details, and the facts. Once a child has completed kindergarten through sixth grade, before their thirteenth birthday, they can matriculate to various educational options.

Students will have already mastered the basics of reading, writing, communication, and arithmetic (few will ever need to know algebra or higher math, and shouldn't be forced to learn it). They should be given appropriate personality and aptitude assessments, then advised of the best options that are most suitable for persons with specific types of profiles. Students, along with their parents or guardians should mull over the results of the assessments, and then decide on the best educational course a child should take. As a child matures, and decides to change educational objectives, a new course should be plotted with the consent of the learner.

The education system is failing because it continues to protect the turf of educationalists, rather than to embrace the pervasiveness of technology and to harness its best applications. Teachers and professors need not fear losing their jobs to on-line education brought directly to students' wristwatch computer companions. Children will continue to require guidance on how to get along with others, how to make sensible decisions, how to stay out of trouble, and how to evolve into positive adults who contribute to bettering their environment and society. Teachers will be able to teach processes and become mentors, rather than to be prisoners of the old school or current pedagogies of regurgitation, wrote memorization, testing, and classroom management.

We are losing our children, not because learning is not inherently interesting, but because the school system has made learning boring or too demanding, creating one "winner" for every nine "losers." The institution of education turns off nine students for every one who remains tuned in. It's not that our students want to fail, but rather they are failing because the educational system fails them. Our school system turns eager and curious minds into self-doubting, fearful, learning avoidant, unhappy, and emotionally damaged teenagers, who become dysfunctional adults, who then raise more out-of-synch children to repeat the cycle again, and so on.

America is great, not because of its educational system, but in spite of it. The great strides in knowledge, discovery, and invention have not come as a direct result of compulsory education, but as the consequence of elective learning that is accomplished by individuals who sought alternatives to the herding strategy and obstacle course evaluation paradigm of teaching that is prevalent in the educational system. The sure thing our education system consistently achieves is the social conditioning of our children into mindless consumers, whose self-image depends on mass media marketing to define value and worth, where their lives become empty unless they can identify with a brand name, a team, and a changing fad. If that's how our society wants to waste the potential of our youth, by turning them from excited and curious learners to seekers of packaged answers, then woe be to our civilization as we plant our own destruction.

It is not too late to turn things around after generations of failure. But our educational bureaucracy is ingrained with career egotists who feel their intellectual superiority and high test scores enable them to dictate what's best for our children. These architects of our educational system understand little of what motivates children to learn, and less of what is necessary for children to feel fulfilled and successful. All these curriculum experts know is how to dump more and more facts on minds that will retain less than 5% of everything that is ever learned in school. Instead, students will turn more and more to computer technology to find the answers and facts that they need to succeed in their everyday lives. Consequently, when our children's learning curve from enhanced technology intersects with classroom teaching pedagogies, and their desire for personalized learning exceeds their willingness to attend class, there will be a revolt and an educational revolution. The old ways and current pedagogies will be forced aside, as a new era of individualized learning shall prevail, with or without the participation of educationalists.

If students learn what is personally important to them, while learning about the world, society, and their environment, then they will feel more satisfied and fulfilled with a purposeful education. Let's begin to convince our educationalists and politicians that our society will be vastly improved if we trust our children enough to open the gates to the corrals, and let our children run. Let them experience the exhilaration of moving their own feet to their hearts content, instead of being herded to as mindless followers to the slaughterhouse of a purposeless consumerist life that is devoid of a sense of community or care for the world they must live in. No, it's still not too late to change the educational paradigm. It's just too unlikely. And that's too bad for every child who must endure the feeling of failure and punishment for learning.

# CHAPTER TWO – EDUCATIONAL POLICIES

There's good reason the U.S. public education system is turning out students who fall far behind the rest of the westernized world in useful facts, knowledge, and mental processes. Let's point the blame where it really belongs; not with insufficient tax monies expended, nor with poorly trained teachers, or demotivated students, but squarely on the backs of the curriculum designers whose choices limit students' freedom to learn information that is practical and reality based. Mass media and other social conditioning institutions has detracted our youth from emphasizing learning, personal development and civic responsibility to escapism, fame, sports, and greed. We must re-think our national obsession with escapism, and make our students more responsible for their own educational choices. When students are permitted to The American public education system has become another employment protection program for a small group of textbook publishers, authors, bureaucrats and administrators who milk the system for on-going personal career security and profits. Students and schools just happen to be the convenient and legitimizing vehicle for "business as usual" at educational institutions and related industries.

In order for students to learn, they must first be instilled with a thirst for learning; supported by sufficient and appropriate materials and tools for learning; and properly mentored and taught by dedicated teachers who believe in the purpose of their work, that of bettering our future through fostering a better educated, more creative, more inquisitive and more responsible citizenry, students who later become successful and well-adjusted adults. When students concentrate on learning about issues they find personally interesting, they automatically become motivated and their achievements become meaningful testaments to their actual learning and understanding.

The old system of rote memorization, the 3 "Rs", and being tested on the "mechanics" of subjects rather than the "processes" involved in discovery does not prepare our students for the real world. Consequently, students with college degrees are told by employers to forget what they've learned in school, and be trained to company standards and regimens in accordance to both the formal and informal organizational structures and cultures. Where do students get a head start on reality lessons? Certainly not from school, and less from popular television so-called reality shows.

Here's what our public education institutions need to do, beginning with yesterday:

1.     Lower mandatory "general education" age limit to 14 because almost all building blocks and fundamental knowledge are already achieved by this age; the typical high school curriculum is a regurgitation of material that should have been properly learned and committed to memory during

formulative years.  Forcing teenagers to re-learn the same materials is boring and often results in higher drop out rates, that if otherwise challenged with more "electives," practical information, and reality-based subjects, more teens would develop a potentially life long thirst for discovery and knowledge.

There are many teens who become experts at computing and programming, who surpass their teachers' abilities with new technologies, yet the school systems continues to utilize old and outdating teaching methods that do little to motivate students to think for themselves and to make good decisions about their own lives.  It has been repeatedly demonstrated that idle minds make for active hands, and it's no wonder so many unchallenged and bored teens turn to destructive handiworks.

2.      Mandatory "trade" or "career" emphasis and job training between 14-16 will better prepare teens for adulthood responsibilities.  Education should not only be theoretical, but the information should have practical applicability in the real world; otherwise we are failing to prepare our youth for a lifetime of work, learning, and responsibilities.  If we don't instill practicum in addition to curriculum, how can we expect our teens to build the habits and knowledge of the working world that they are expected to master upon matriculation and graduation?

We teach them to cut up frogs in basic biology classes, but don't give students any practical knowledge on how to cut up chicken into pieces that can be easily cooked. We teach students about acceleration and inertia, but fail to give graphic examples of its demonstration as the outcome of car crashes. We teach human anatomy, but don't discuss how exercise and dancing are interactions of interdependent systems in the human body that seeks homeostasis. Unfortunately, students are left to discover the true realities in life after school, because school knowledge is generally information with little applicability in their daily lives, and it shouldn't be that way.

3.      Voluntary education after age 16, and age of consent is crucial; otherwise the extra years of irresponsibility and weaning weakens our youth's self-image and demotivates them from becoming masters of their own fates. In most nations, particularly in the Third World, a 14 year old is already expected to take on responsibilities for working and helping their families. When they display sufficient maturity, they are permitted to marry and to raise families. Discouraging work and responsibility between the ages of 16 and 18 serves to retard the development of a sense of personal motivation, goals, maturity, and responsibility for oneself and their surroundings. This extended play period is not healthy because the majority of teens at this age, particularly females, have matured both physically and emotionally and are ready to take on the full fledge self-image as adults.

As long as we treat them as kids, they will act like children. If society prepares them for self-sufficiency and grants them the rights of adulthood, there will be far less teens in trouble, locked up in prisons, and escaping into hedonistic binges of booze, sex, and drug abuse. Every individual matures at different rates, depending upon the interaction of their genetic predisposition and their family/social environment. Anyone who feels they have attained intellectual and emotional maturity should be allowed to demonstrate their capabilities through various measures. If they pass the tests, they should be considered matured and responsible adults.

Certainly, our bloodthirsty society considers 10 year old children as adults for incarceration and possibly the death penalty when through their immaturity and poor judgment, they commit heinous crimes. Yet society won't allow our teens to embrace the social responsibilities of adulthood. There's some blatant legal and social hypocrisy there. Let's set aside traditional ideas and norms regarding maturity, and change to a reasonable paradigm that could work.

4.      Greater individual choice in the selection of coursework and specialization will enable students to feel empowered and engage them in a personal educational process that will have life long benefits, both to themselves and to society at large. Students tend to do poorly or fail classes where the subject matter is not interesting to them

personally; and to excel at those subjects that interest them. We should allow students to develop a passion for discovery and knowledge, a motivation that can only be nurtured by allowing personal choice to alter the educational plan, replacing a mandatory read and rote school curriculum that has consistently proven itself to fail most of our students.

Our students are consumers of educational products, and they should be allowed reasonable choices as consumers and not have forced education jammed down their throats. If we continue to force feed facts down our children's throats, they will develop stomach aches and heartburn instead of mental insights. Let them think for themselves and make informed choices from the beginning and not only at the end of the educational process, and they will bloom like the prettiest flowers in well-irrigated educational soil.

Elimination of "required courses" that are not applicable to students' career plans allows students to concentrate on developing expertise in areas of their interests and passion. We insist that our students receive a broad and general education, covering the breadth of human knowledge; but in real life, the best paying careers require expertise and specialization. The body of knowledge has increased on geometric proportions since only a generation ago, and the amount of information we expect our students to learn and retain has generally exceeded their attention span, memory capacity, and interests. We need to reduce the number of required courses, and increase career related classes to improve motivation and the development of expertise that is required by our rapidly changing technologies and world.

5.　　Greater use and integration of on on-line courses still drags far behind its potential due to career and turf protection that is endemic to the educational industry. Why must students be forced to learn all coursework in classroom settings, where other students who are bored, attention-starved, or poorly behaved can reduce the learning opportunity for quieter students? It's been 60 years since the beginning of the Internet, and about 20 years since the personal computer made the Internet available to average people, yet its use as an educational tool has been painstakingly slow.

While entertaining and socially stimulating at times, the Internet has been relegated to on-line shopping, auctions, chat, email, porn, and dating. Instead, the Internet should be the universal link in cyberspace between eager students and dedicated professors worldwide, bringing a broader and more realistic educational forum to students at-large. The software and hardware have been in place for the past decade; however the greatest resistance to embracing and fully utilizing the technology has come from the educational sector for fear of losing their jobs. It is now possible for renowned professors to lecture on their subject fields, and have millions of students interact with other professors who can work one-on-one to explain the concepts to those who need additional help.

Wouldn't education improve when every student has equal access to the best minds in the human race, and not be limited solely to teachers who are good at babysitting disruptive students with behavioral problems? Let's embrace and fully utilized the technology of learning. Instead of a few slow MAC computers in each classroom, every student should be assigned a laptop with access to all the major research databases in the world. And when computer miniaturization reduces laptops to card size, then there will be no excuse for ignorance.

6.     More appropriate and world-class curricula are essential to augment and harness the basic power of the 3 R's. Every human predicament requires the use of at least one or two of the 3 R's to provide constructive solutions. After students achieve competence in the basics, which is typically attainable by age 12, curricula should be advanced which challenge students to apply their basic knowledge in logical and strategic methods to problem solve, or to create innovative concepts. Let's emphasize thinking in addition to learning, as both are essential parts of the other. Without the one, the other withers.

7.　　Universal educational standards that make sense are urgently needed. The current body of curriculum specialists have generally missed the boat on the type of knowledge that is essential to build a better world, happier and more fulfilled human beings, and lessen violence and warfare in the world. They seem to feel that knowledge for knowledge sake is sufficient justification for forcing facts down the throats of our youth, our futures. It is not enough to educate. Education must be appropriate, useful, practical, and fulfilling the purpose of improving individuals and humanity; otherwise why bother. We might as well be in the Dark Ages if what is taught does little to improve the lot of humanity.

Even were the myriad of educational experts to agree on anything, and even were these educational reform ideas to be accepted by the government and school boards around the nation, it will still take another generation to implement. The problem lies in the reality that with quickly changing technology that is designed to eliminate human effort from the work equation, coupled with cheap overseas labor that is as good or better than our domestic technical, skilled and unskilled labor pools, is what we're teaching our students going to prepare them for surviving the future?

We don't have a generation to plan and implement practical changes. We should have, could have, and would have made substantive educational reforms a generation ago, were our politicians, bureaucrats and specialists not so indebted to special interest lobbyists who represent corporate book publishers, school construction conglomerates, mass-media giants, and an educational system that is designed to turn out socially conditioned copycats who compete to consume brand names, instead of self-actualized human beings who seek to better themselves, their communities, the environment and the world at large. Shame on public education and all its policy makers.

# CHAPTER THREE – TEACHING LESS

*Why would anyone want to be a teacher nowadays?*

It doesn't pay to be a teacher nowadays. Dangers lurk from threats, assaults, and career ending false accusations from disgruntled students and dysfunctional parents. Take the recent case of a high school coach in Los Angeles, who luckily was acquitted of charges he had sodomized a high school basketball player. Now his parents want to file a civil suit against the school district. Stories abound. In recent decades, there appears to be a marked increase in the percentage of people who are willing to destroy good teachers' lives so they can sue school districts for the big bucks. How many good teachers are falsely accused and convicted by the system? Surely some who are convicted on circumstantial evidence and false testimony are innocent, but the guilty ones should go to jail... no sympathy from me.

Teachers are being blamed for the ills of society. Their careers are always in a tenuous position. Their pay is relatively low, stress often high, and their classrooms can be dangerous and sometimes life threatening places. Five years of college and one year of internship starts teachers with a salary that is less than that paid to police officers, who also have dangerous jobs. More than ever before, teachers find themselves being unfairly cornered into the dubious position as scapegoats for society's failures and subjected to subterfuge by both students and parents. Teachers need to learn how to better manage staff and students, and to read the nuances that are present in classroom relationships that can result in distrust, misunderstanding, and conspiracy. The teaching profession is filled with potential traps, legal "catch 22's", relationship distortions with staff, students, and parents that can lead to misperceptions and complaints. The liability aspects are great, and the potential for false accusations is always present. Teachers are expected to be responsible for parenting and character building in addition to procuring higher test scores from their diverse student populations. Yet, teachers are impotent to affect much of anything if students, parents, and staff are not cooperative. Teachers are held legally, criminally, and financially responsible for the outcomes of activities, known or unknown to them, in their classrooms, and they are held to a higher moral code than parents, politicians and the police.

Being a teacher nowadays requires a certain degree of "gumption"... dedication, courage, patience, persistence, and forgiveness. Teachers now occupy an occupation that is constantly criticized, evaluated, microscopically monitored, subjected to undue financial and legal liabilities, public suspicion, and occasionally unsympathetic and unreasonable administrative and political pressure to create high achievement from children of dysfunctional families in a failing civilization. Teachers are being assaulted on many fronts, physically, mentally, and emotionally, and they are becoming the scapegoats for society's ills and faults, while politicians shift the blame for the consequences of poverty and racism to teachers.

Why do teachers need to do a better job? And what can we realistically expect teachers to embrace as their responsibilities for the mental, emotional, and moral development of our children? First, teachers need administrative, procedural, and legal protection from misbehaving and overly aggressive students, and irrational and dysfunctional parents. Teachers must be shielded from false accusations and resultant litigation, and even criminal charges that result when police are called unnecessarily and unfairly to taint the good reputation of teachers just because a few notorious examples of teacher misconduct have been in the news. Statistics prove that 99.9% of teachers are not molesters, but instead are leaders in their classrooms, who teach and nurture our students for a better future. Certainly, no one gets rich from teaching kids.

School administrators owe it to the teaching profession to diplomatically handle all complaints that question teacher professionalism, and should come to the defense of teachers, rather than to abandon them, or to disassociate when media attention is focused on their schools. Every year, countless numbers of teachers have to endure incidents where they become victims of violence, verbal and physical abuse, false accusation as perpetrator of all sorts of misconduct; from yelling at students, verbally threatening students, inappropriately touching students, ineffective teaching strategies, insensitivity to demanding parents, and the list goes on. This is a very disturbing trend in America, where teachers are subjected to lingering doubts about their personal reputations as they are under constant suspicion and often have little defense against total fabrications besides the admission by accusers of errors, misinterpretations, misperceptions or outright lies. And how often do false accusers admit their wrong doings? Rarely is it a crime.

Teachers need to be advised and warned not to be so forthright in their classrooms, and to withhold examples of personal opinions and experiences. To prevent potential mistakes in class that may set them up for future allegations and litigations, teachers should document any potentially controversial remarks they might make in the course of getting through the day. They must be able to come to class each day with a clear state of mind so they may give their best effort as teachers to help our children to improve their mental and emotional development, even though it's unfair to expect teachers to provide a completely safe classroom environment due to the lack of respect, and aggressiveness that many students display toward teachers and authority nowadays. It's not fair for society to expect teachers to be parent, police, and psychologist, without giving them rights and the necessary tools to do more than teach.

Many classroom situations cause high anxiety not only for students but for teachers. These occupational conditions contribute to setbacks in teacher's physical and mental health due to high levels of responsibility and liability that their classes, including disruptive students who may be emotionally disturbed, create in stress and drama for everyone. Teachers often don't feel safe in their own classrooms due to unstable environmental factors such as unpredictable student actions and behaviors. Consequently, teaching demands a new emphasis on dealing with the behavioral peculiarities and needs of students, parents and staff that takes away from the focus on helping children to learn. Even the most patient and humble teachers can get hurt due to the lessening of positive circumstances in the teaching environment where they can enjoy a sense of safety, accomplishment, and fulfillment. Teachers seek confidence in the trenches where there is a constant level of challenge, lost of respect, and distractions to their effectiveness due to a lack of support and understanding of the current teaching environment by politicians, parents, and administrators. Rarely if ever is the issue of problems confronting teachers mentioned in the news media or by politicians, which are rarely dealt with in teaching credential programs and by prominent teacher unions, except during election years.

Especially in the field of special education, behavioral problems are often exacerbated by staff. In cases where instructional aides are used, too often they are rarely trained and may have developed the habit of yelling and triggering students to "act out." It's challenging enough that many students are often anxious due to the unpredictable environment of being at school, in classes that are potentially "explosive", often changing (students are transferred in and out), and where they are expected to be "mainstreamed" to keep up with the "regular" students in both academics and behavior for the entire school day. These expectations oftentimes exceed the individual emotionally disturbed or disabled student's ability to retain self-control, and one consequence is they explode into various inappropriate behaviors. Having these types of students in the same environment magnifies the probability of negative behaviors, as one student sets off another, and at times, when staff contributes to heightening the emotional temperature in the classroom, the results are predictable... chaos. We see this principle occurring among the "normal" population, as frustrated and angry citizens riot in the streets when authority is used excessively. In the classroom, the same microcosm exist. When teachers and staff attempt to apply authority excessively, there's a tendency for rebellion against order because students want and need a sense of control over their lives due to their own confusion, uncertainties, and insecurities. While they may need more structure, too many in the teaching profession confuse "structure" with "authoritarianism", resulting in the creation of classroom environments that are not conducive to learning and growth.

Fortunately, the vast majority of teachers and para-educators are sensitive and sensible in their desire and approach to helping students, but occupational frustration with changing attitudes in school often takes its toll on the patience level required of teaching staff.

The majority of para-educators are aides instead of teachers because they tend to have little training and education. They attempt to do their jobs based primarily on their experiences in life and with raising their own children. How can we expect aides to parent emotionally disturbed or disabled children when their own parenting practices may be inadequate? A requisite for teaching special children is to be very patient, and to speak softly, using directive questioning that clearly defines the alternatives of decision making choices to ensure that students are making desirable mental and emotional connections. People who deal with special children need to realize that they're special for many reasons, and to be more sympathetic. Instructional assistants can either improve, hinder, or disrupt the teaching effort in the classroom. Many "veterans" are overly protective of their turf and routines, and they tend to resist direction from teachers, especially new teachers to "their" classroom. Teachers oftentimes find themselves trying to teach not only the students, but also instructional aides who may not know how to act, and whose interactions may be detrimental to the emotional health of students.

Those courageous and dedicated souls who remain in the teaching profession from true desire to make positive contributions to the development of children should receive all the support that the "system" can give; from parents, administrators, politicians and students. Certainly, the job is not an easy one; the pay is mediocre, responsibilities and liabilities are great, and gratitude is more often a personalized phenomenon rather than displays of appreciation from others, whether parents, staff, administrators, or politicians.

Who will speak out for teachers? So far, no charismatic leader has taken up the causes of teachers, and until legislators begin to think more pragmatically rather than politically, teachers will continue to receive less respect, gratification and support, and instead will continue to be blamed for our society's misgivings and for the shortcomings in their profession. Anyone who has the heart to continue teaching should be commended. All others beware the traps of being a teacher. As a former teacher of severely emotionally disturbed middle school students, I had taken a sabbatical from the profession to safeguard my life, freedom, and sanity, not because of the kids, but due to a conspiracy of three assistants who felt I was a threat to their comfort zone and program of kicking back, shoving students around, yelling, and setting them off. They were people who were collecting checks because they lacked other marketable talents, in my opinion. I suspect more teachers will decide to leave teaching careers, further exacerbating an already serious teacher shortage that will be accentuated by Proposition 98, and impending retirements within the next five to ten years, while a relative few opt to tackle the challenges of teaching.

Who can justly blame teachers for leaving an increasingly politicized and demonized profession that is rife with potential litigation and personal liability for alleged criminal and civil acts or omissions?  And how fair is it to blame teachers for pervasive low test scores from dysfunctional and demotivated children from hostile and negative environments, especially where poverty, crime, and lack of adult supervision is prevalent?  It's not fair, and teachers who are fed up are quitting by record numbers, while teacher tenure rapidly decreases in response to the growing environment of disempowerment, political and bureaucratic manipulation and societal insensitivity and blame.  My hat's off to all dedicate teachers who can survive.  As for me, I'm planning to throw in the towel by the end of the year if not sooner.  And the sad fact is I believe the vast preponderance of the children who I've attempted to teach genuinely like me, though I've been warned by staff not to treat them so nice, or they'd take advantage of me.  But from my perspective, I get more cooperation from children by giving them kindness, than by being a demanding authoritarian.  In fact, one of my ex-SED classes loved me so much, I could not visit the school site, because they would run out of their room to hug me. They also painted "Wu Tang Clan" in the front of their classroom, to express their love and appreciation.

I cannot visit them, because it would give them false hope that the system will change any time soon. Perhaps we need to teach more kindness in university teacher preparation programs. If we cannot instill love and concern in those who are entrusted to guide our future generations, then our civilization is doomed, even without the scourge of terrorism. I am very disheartened by the state of our teaching profession, as I feel we're turning out novices who are ill prepared to deal with the hard knocks that face them. At the least, we owe them a warning.

# CHAPTER FOUR – EDUCATION GRANTS

A Concept Paper for ACE:  Achieving Community Excellence Program (This proposals incorporates previously stated goals and proposed solutions)

Executive Summary

Impoverished, ignored, and immigrant children usually perform at lower tiers of academic excellence when compared to other "mainstream" middle-class groups.  The underprivileged educational stew has been stirred and stirred, new ingredients tried, and the political temperature cranked up several notches during election years.  SAT scores have slowly inched up over the past 5 years; however, this may reflect changes in the test that help to improve scores, or greater numbers of students resorting to SAT preparatory courses, or teachers helping their students to become better test takers.

Regardless of what public education has become, it certainly is not anticipating the profound changes that are rapidly taking place in society due to technology.  Computers are not properly utilized in the classrooms, and emphasizing repetition, memorization and test taking performance will not turn out the type of people who will be able to think, make appropriate decisions, be employable, or survive the next 20 years. As non-traditional students graduate from high school (or college) and enter the work world, much of their knowledge will be useless, either because technology will make their education irrelevant or obsolete, or their technical expertise will find greater employment at one-tenth the salary in a foreign country.

The public education curriculum primarily addresses the 3 R's, and does not focus on the real world application of knowledge. Traditional educational pedagogy creates nine failures for every success due to the enforcement of an antiquated grading system that robs students of their sense of self worth, curiosity and discovery, and replaces it with insecurity and the willingness to accept other people's values and norms. If the public school system's goal is to create followers or failures, then it has been highly successful. Students who are bored or turned off by school become our delinquents and criminals. Those who become comfortable as part of the herd easily find their niches in corporations that seek mindless "yes men" to obey directives of demanding bosses whose primary concern is profit and personal recognition. The lucky ten percent who graduate with a positive self image fill in middle management positions to lead and manipulate mediocre classmates who form the herds, or some become the professional status quo maintainers of the hierarchical socio-economic system that supports the fortune and fame of the elites.

The privileged children of the elites enjoy the education of private academies, which prepare them for Ivy League universities and corporate boardrooms. All American presidents have had "pedigree" backgrounds, have graduated from upper crust universities, and have had the support of financiers who benefit from government contracts or subsidies. The glass ceiling of success is triple thick for impoverished minorities, immigrants,
and our ignored children who comprise an invisible underground segment of our society. The most disenfranchised, discouraged, and demeaned groups of our children suffer most in our public schools. Unless failing curriculum, pedagogy and purpose are fixed, society can expect few of our discouraged children will rise above the glass ceiling to contribute new perspectives to better our world. Perhaps that is the real purpose of our public education system in our class conscious society.

Vision

The world is not fair. It never has been, and never will be. Children born into lives of misfortune must struggle and fight their way out of their circumstances of destitute, with few positive examples in their immediate environment, and little support from their schools. Impoverished and immigrant students are usually faced with negative experiences that condition them to expect little from society, school and other people. The public schools system forces them to accept the judgment of others in place of their own ability to make beneficial decisions. Those who refuse or can't fit the educational mold often rebel or get into trouble with their classmates, teachers, parents or authorities.

The issues are not about rights or fairness, though they may well be. The issues are about saving our children and consequently, helping to make a better society for us all. The public schools system is slow to change, and has basically remained the same generation to generation. Knowledge has been incremental, and now our children are expected to know much more than their processors, further multiplying opportunities to fail in our schools. In some rare cases, individual teachers or programs have made significant contributions to motivate students to higher achievements; however, those successes are almost never adopted or implemented system wide because students who are products of public education aren't supposed to be successful for their socio-economic class.

A highly successful public education system may over time begin to threaten and challenge the excellence of elitist proprietary schools, which would make the unequal system of class-based superiority a weakened institution. We all know that there is a limited amount of space reserved at the top. In many respects, public education serves four purposes:

1) to turn out followers who rarely think for themselves or question authority; 2) to reinforce the structure of privilege for certain social classes; 3) to have a place to put our children during the hours when parents must work, and; 4) to protect the careers of educators and administrators. Politicians also use the issue of a failing public education system as political fodder, while they send their own children to privileged private schools and universities. They rarely know how to fix the failing public schools system, or sincerely care to fix it at all after elections. The people elected or appointed to boards of education have little teaching experience and possess narrow perspectives on student needs.

The solutions for fixing a failing public education system are simple. First students must be motivated to learn. They must be willing and able to learn in an environment that is conducive to learning. When children from diverse backgrounds, challenging neighborhoods, and dysfunctional family environments are placed in classrooms, it is impossible for them to achieve at optimal levels. Individuals learn differently at different paces; however, most coursework is designed to be completed at the pace set by textbooks. Those who don't keep up are judged to be poor students or failures, and become disinclined from learning. Many children attend school for social aspects instead of academic purpose, especially those who lose interest in learning due to poor grades. Certainly, developing social skills is important in everyone lives, and is usually essential in career and interpersonal relations; however, few schools emphasize constructive social development as a part of teaching pedagogy. And even fewer schools understand how to use social reinforcers to encourage and motivate their students to higher levels of learning and achievement.

The second solution to improve learning is to provide adequate and appropriate materials and technology. The third solution to entice students to learn is to reinforce their natural curiosity and desire for discovery. The fourth solution to enhance learning is to implement sensible and positive teaching strategies. The fifth improvement to the learning environment is to remove negative reinforcers, such as the punitive traditional grading system that is based upon comparative test grades alone. The sixth precondition of effective learning is designing study programs that address individual needs, interests and abilities that are appropriately paced to reflect personal choice and diversity. The seventh solution to repairing the public schools system is to create classrooms where students can develop mutual respect, tolerance, decision-making, positive social interaction, and self expression without feeling fear, intimidation or pressure to conform to social norms.

## Purpose

This proposal recognizes public education's resistance to change due to various reasons, some obvious and others arguably controversial. A model after school program, Achieving Community Excellence, or ACE, is proposed to emphasize the academic and social development of students in the context of improving themselves and their communities. As long as our underprivileged communities turn out leaders of gangs instead of civic leaders, both institutions of public schools and family life are failing. The fiscal crisis that faces government at all levels severely limits the amount of individualized teaching that can be afforded in public schools, therefore private and non-profit funding must be sought to bridge this widening gap.

The ACE program is intended to be a demonstration project that combines sensible and effective teaching solutions as described in the preceding vision statement's seven solutions. ACE is designed as an after school program to be held on school campuses, as funding permits. After completion of the program's first year, subsequent to positive evaluations by students, parents, their communities, teachers and the education profession, proposals will seek to expand the scope and breadth of ACE.

## Goals

The fundamental goals of ACE are to augment the positive aspects of the public schools education paradigm, while reversing the negative outcomes from public schools inadequacies for impoverished, immigrant, and ignored students. ACE will focus primarily on rekindling students' curiosity and desire for discovery and learning about themselves as individuals, about others as part of their schools and communities, and about their unfolding future.

The ACE program may be applicable at any level of education, but would be appropriate at middle grades, before attitudes and behaviors become habitual and oftentimes irreversible. Instilling a thirst for learning, development of self-motivation, encouragement of self-confidence, and the realization of appropriate and effective interpersonal relations must not wait until high school years, where peer pressure often define anti-social norms. The ACE program must not be viewed as another diversionary after school babysitting program whose purpose is primarily to keep children supervised and off the streets while their parents are at work, which would result in little if any substantive progress. The ACE project is meant to make a positive difference, and to demonstrate to parents, educators and politicians that small positive changes can have large pervasive beneficial outcomes.

## Objectives

Students will be encouraged, mentored and motivated to exercise their personal options to discover individual interests, and to pursue those areas of interest in depth for optimally retentive learning. The teaching-learning environment will be organized to emphasize rational decision-making within the context of individual choice and group dynamics. Real world situations will provide case studies from which knowledge and social skills can be integrated to create practical and realistic solutions. Skills learned through the ACE program will be transferable to students' regular classroom learning experiences to improve their comprehension, behavior, participation and performance on normal evaluation criteria.

Primary objectives will include improvements in students' ability to:

1. Read and comprehend complex material.
2. Correctly complete math operations and applications.
3. Write sensibly, legibly, and concisely.
4. Think creatively, rationally, and positively.
5. Analyze patterns, abstractions, and associations.
6. Make logical and good decisions based upon situational facts.
7. Act appropriately and respectfully in present circumstances.
8. Speak intelligently with effective articulation and communication.
9. Remember, recall, repeat, and summarize knowledge and facts.
10. Compare and contrast data from examples applicable in reality.
11. Listen; follow instructions and directions of knowledge providers.
12. Develop a desire to learn as an avenue to satisfy curiosity.

13. Ask well-formulated questions based upon deep thinking.

14. Consider plausible options, alternatives and solutions.

15. Get along well with others in cooperative group activities.

16. Respect authority figures who provide assistance and guidance.

17. Be trustworthy and dependable by delivering on commitments.

18. Accept personal responsibility for results, errors and outcomes.

19. Obey school and classroom rules designed to balance freedoms.

20. Desire to succeed and strive for individual life-long learning.

## Strategies

Various effective techniques will be implemented to maximize student learning and to instill positive attitude changes, among which will be:

1. A proactive and motivational classroom management plan that guides student behaviors, rather than reacting to inappropriate behaviors and rewarding disruptive students with attention.

2. An integrated approach that addresses the entire learning experience, which rejects the myth of subject dysfunctionality (i.e., poor at math and science). Encourage students to excel at subjects of personal interest and value.

3. Multi-tiered and individualized pace of learning that eliminates herding of students who possess varying abilities into the failure and standardized paradigms.

4. Modeling by mentor teachers, who provide positive examples of graduated step learning, and inspire students to excel.

5. Hands on participatory learning with unlimited support materials to improve individual study plans.

6. Inspiration and motivation through interesting materials taught by inspiring teachers in highly motivating approaches.

7. Emphasizing expertise and excellence versus irrelevant and useless facts and mediocrity.

8. Recognition for individual achievement and contribution to the betterment of one's community and school with scholarships.

9. Grading and evaluation system based upon individual learning, and not test taking ability alone. Assessment will emphasize student improvement, application of knowledge, decision-making and problem solving, instead of memorizing random facts, figures, dates, and unrelated data. Content, rather than form will be encouraged, as an insightful discovery that leads to personal growth must not be downgraded on account of a few spelling or grammatical oversights. An unintended negative consequence of the traditional grading system results when teachers miss the

creativity, competency, and actual learning that takes place when they focus on grammatical perfection, where an A+ paper becomes a "C" due to a few misspellings or grammatical errors.

10. Homework is voluntary to supplement curiosity, discovery and desire to excel in learning. Homework must not be busy work to generate more grades for grades sake.

11. Simplicity and honesty must be emphasized, as complexity should be avoided when simplicity would suffice.

12. Straight forward approach that eliminates confusing jargon and contradictory materials. Conceptual frameworks are learned in terms that make sense to students, who may pick up jargon as their comprehension matures.

13. Appropriate penalties for disruptions, beginning with student conference, reasoning, retention plan, suspension or expulsion.

14. Parental participation to support educational objectives by cooperating with teachers.

15. Parental supervision of students' study time while at home, rather than parental abrogation and sole reliance on teachers.

16. Religious tolerance in a historical context, as part of freedoms guaranteed by the U.S. Constitution.

The concept of "God" must not become a "bad word" that is totally avoided in intellectual and social discussions because real world relations are greatly influenced and altered by religious intolerance and ignorant stereotypes. Secondary strategies will emphasize resolving inherent contradictions between lessons taught in school versus real world success paradigms, as:

1. A good education does not guarantee a well paying career, as networking and well-placed connections increase the probability of being hired for good jobs. Realistic educational and career assessments must be disclosed to students so they may have a realistic basis to plan their future goals.

2. Listening and following directions is required of low-skilled and mundane jobs, but creativity and good decision making are highly rewarded and personally fulfilling in well paying careers.

3. Authority determines the standards for inmates, but successful people define their own standards and goals in the real world.

4. Comparing oneself to others set comfortable and predictable norms, but true success comes from doing your own thing and being happy with what you personally accomplish for yourself.

5. Conforming to social norms may be necessary to survive certain situations at work, church or school.

Real freedom comes from choosing your own path and then going your own way.

6. Excellence in performance and testing demonstrates one's ability to figure out what others expect; consequently, work smarter and not harder, and enjoy the time and effort saved.

7. Socializing in traditional classroom settings disrupt others who want to learn, but astute social skills and popularity translates to success, monetary rewards and leadership in the real world.

8. Talking while learning is normally viewed as not attending to tasks; however in our technology and profit driven world, the ability to multi-task, work effectively with multiple distractions, and to make and communicate clear decisions that others are willing to adopt are functions of effective leadership.

9. Teachers constantly admonish students to be more serious and not to joke around in class, but appropriately timed levity helps to improve group dynamics, satisfaction and productivity.

10. "Don't be the class clown," is a mantra of frustrated teachers. In real life, appropriate humor is rewarding and attractive.

ACE needs the committed services of mentor teachers who are experts in their academic fields, adept at transferring knowledge and motivating students to learn, as a life long desire and attitude of personal discovery. Creativity, adeptness in evaluating students' abilities, and communicating constructive learning strategies are essential teaching attributes. ACE does not believe in teaching to the text, but in student comprehension, personal discovery, and self-actualization. Each student should develop the goal to excel at particular arenas of knowledge, and to focus on developing their own expertise that would be suitable for their grade level.

Curriculum

A broader exposure to knowledge that is essential in the real world should be pursued in order for students to recognize the interdependency and interrelated disciplines, particularly as applied in careers. While deep examination would not normally begin at the middle and high school levels, the ACE after school demonstration project intends to show that students are highly capable of pursuing any academic field in some depth. Students who are interested and sufficiently encouraged are likely to expend the time and energy required by excellence, if adequate guidance and support is provided by their schools and teachers. The following fields of knowledge are ripe for discovery and inclusion as supplemental study.

1.    Curriculum reforms must emphasize practical education that applies foundational skills in reading, writing and mathematics to real world problems, in preparation for living and working in a technological world, while ingraining social morals to enhance civility and societal stability.

2.    Cultural enrichment
- international relations, conflict resolution & partnership
- patriotism, legal system, politics, and humanitarianism
- effects of globalization, regionalism and centralism
- religious, cultural, and historical perspectives

3.    Important Aspects of the Real World
- economics and finance
- world banking system
- international trade
- investments
- marketing

4.    Science
- physics, chemistry, biology, anatomy, & astronomy
- pharmacology and molecular biology
- immunology and health (disease prevention)
- genetics and human genomics
- microbiology and bioengineering
- environmental sciences, meteorology, seismology

5.  Technology
    - computer miniaturization and applications
    - energy and alternative energies
    - engineering (all areas)
    - architecture and building materials innovation
    - nanotechology and robotics
    - artificial intelligence
    - biotechnology
6.  Social and political
    - treating and healing dysfunctional personalities
    - opinion research and political policies
    - decision-making techniques and strategies
    - humanistic development and evolution
    - peaceful conflict resolution and diplomacy
    - globalization consequences
    - global distribution of wealth and resources
    - assessment of learning should be accurate and meaningful.  It is not enough to have students mark Scantron computerized test grading sheets.

Students should be challenged to demonstrate their individual command and understanding of knowledge through practical application to real world scenarios that interest them.

a.  Standardization
   - testing application knowledge, not memory data
   - non-punitive grading system
   - self-assessment
b.  Individualization
   - pace of learning
   - personal interest elective courses
   - decision-making strategies
   - self-directedness

Educational reforms must become depoliticized. Politicians should not pass legislation without adequate studies by expert panels of educators that justify particular changes. Educational funding formulas must not be subject to partisan politics. Teachers must not blamed for lower student scores without proper individual assessment of students' baseline performance prior to testing, as well as subsequent to testing. Student should be given proper credit for their degree of improvement, particularly impoverished, immigrant and ignored students who struggle to keep up with others.

Pedagogy

Urgent changes are required to enhance educational intent and outcomes, which will significantly improve learning and test scores. Some of the changes needed in the classroom include:

1.  Class size reduction

a. Ratio of 1:15 for average students; 1:10 for gifted students; 1:5 for special needs students, and less than 45 students in lecture hall settings.

b. Team teaching and combining classrooms for lectures.

2. Computer applications

a. Ideal of one terminal per student; minimum of one terminal per 2 students, with laptops preferred.

b. Lesson modules at individualized pace beyond minimal schedule benchmarks.

c. Networking with area schools for group learning.

3. Visual aids

a. More effective use of video and CD educational programs.

b. On-line materials to supplement lecture and texts.

c. Computer media in paperless networked classrooms.

4. Tiered learning groups

a. Eager, fast, and/or gifted learners.

b. Average paced learners.

c. Slow learners/non-behavioral causation.

d. Behavioral dysfunction and post-incarceration.

e. Special education and trainable mentally handicapped.

5.  Diagnostic assessment
    a.  Aptitude and interest inventories at appropriate grades.
    b.  Memory, analytical ability, reasoning skills and creativity
    c.  Learning style, attention and focus propensities

## Support

Teachers and students often feel they are in urban battlefields. More protection is needed by teachers to create safer classrooms.

1.  Protecting teachers
    a.  No law enforcement involvement until after thorough administrative review by school district investigators.
    b.  Referral to law enforcement investigation only after school investigation discovers criminal acts.
    c.  Reasonable teacher self-defense for unprovoked attacks.
    d.  Attorney for teachers must be present during teacher interrogations by administration or law enforcement.

e. Reinstatement of humane physical punishment program below sixth grade, with documented parental consent, and punishment documented by written and video evidence.

2. Classroom management

a. Cameras, recording video, and audio controlled by office.

b. Disrupters escorted out of classrooms by school security.

c. Disrupters subject to behavior management specialists, or psychiatric interventions, and must clear before allowing readmission to class.

3. Managing student misbehaviors

a. Attention seeking and inappropriate speech or actions: Verbal correction, counseling, essay, or apologize.

b. Moderately disruptive language and behaviors:
   - 1st incident = verbal warning; 2nd = detention; 3rd = parent meeting

c. Highly dramatic and disruptive language and behaviors:
   - 1st incident = detention, parent conference; 2nd = suspension

d. Violence, attempted violence, or threats of violence:

- to self = detention, psych intervention, and parent conference.
- to others = detention, suspension or expulsion - depending on severity, administrative investigation, referral to law enforcement for legal action.

e. Suspension must not reward students who act out to get out for free time with other delinquent minors, or time at home to play video games.

f. Expulsion must not reward students who don't care about school, who only seek time away from class to run about.

4. Government and community support

a. Patriotism- flag salute encouraged but not mandatory.

b. Community and school pride for academic excellence.

c. Classroom and school safety for students and teachers who are "at risk" in certain high crime neighborhoods.

d. Political support for education, instead of the illusion of support.

e.   Legal system support of teachers, who currently have few rights and protections, and are subjected to frivolous accusations by disgruntled and vengeful poor students.

Proposed Budget:

$205,000/first year @ $6,833 per student.
$155,000/2nd year @ $5,167 per student.

1.   2 classes of 15 students; two .5 FTE teachers @$80,000/yr.
2.   One administrator who acts as substitute teacher @$45,000/yr.
3.   33 Internet assessable laptop computers @$1500 ea.~ $50,000
4.   33 high speed Internet connections with service @$6,000/yr.
5.   Individualized textbooks @$200 per student = $6,000/yr.
6.   2 classroom rent @$2000/mo = $18,000 per 9 months.

# Evaluation

The ACE demonstration project attempts to promote an integrated education plan to provide field data that supports improving our nation's public education system, particularly where impoverished, immigrant, or ignored students have suffered the consequences of failure orientation promoted by traditional school settings. The ACE emphasis is also for educational funds to give more "bang" and less "gangs" for the buck. We need to build a thirst for knowledge and desire for pursuing success, rather than using an obsolete measuring stick to create nine failures for every single success. We need to put more individual choice in schools, so students can feel empowered to learn what they feel are most relevant and useful in their lives, and not be forced to move with the herd, either too slowly for some, or too fast for others. It's no wonder many students are bored with school, or hate it.

The ACE project will stand up to community, educational, political, parental, bureaucratic and most importantly student evaluation of the basic criteria that justify the ACE program's intent, goals, objectives and actual measurable outcomes. These areas of assessment include the following:

1. Are the educational purpose, vision, and intent satisfied?
   a. Educational purpose can be assessed based upon the content of supplemental coursework and curriculum.
   b. Achievement of intent and vision could be assessed by the choices of elective coursework, survey of student satisfaction and improvement in academic performance.

2. Are the goals and objectives adequately achieved?
   a. Student improvement in basic 3 R's testing.
   b. Student electives contribute to higher motivation and overall improvement in academic performance.
   c. After school program enriches students' lives, and provides a constructive platform for achievement.
   d. School clubs and activities are initiated by students that tackle various school and community issues.
   e. Students' independent learning projects emphasize learning, which also enhances test performance.

3. Are the intervening strategies and curriculum effective?

    a. Sensible and practical curriculum that emphasizes problem solving, creativity, discovery and exploration – not only random memorization of events and dates but actual comprehension and application of concepts to practical real world scenarios.

    b. Appropriate civic and interpersonal lessons in material.

    c. Positive test results, high retention of knowledge and transferable improvement to regular school scores.

    d. Student attitude and behavior.

- respects teachers and authority
- respects and gets along with classmates
- listens intently and speaking appropriately follows instructions and implements directions
- asks for permission, avoids interruptions
- respects quiet needed by others while studying
- talks appropriately to contribute to group projects
- students accept and exhibit personal responsibility

4.     Teacher qualifications and mindset
   a.     Committed to provide a purposeful education to youth.
   b.     High degree of competence in their academic subject.
   c.     Understanding students' needs and motivations.
   d.     Feels teaching is a highly rewarding profession.
   e.     Honest, fair, moral, and impartial character traits.
   f.     Patient, mature, helpful, and friendly personality.
   g.     Engaging, inspiring, and motivating attitude.

## Conclusions

The future of education will be revolutionary. Students will discover that the correlation between future employment benefits and level of educational attainment will be illusory, except in certain high demand professional fields that are not prone to outsourcing to offshore locations. In most cases, a higher education will not be required to perform job functions, but may be required to validate the value of college degrees.

Technology will enhance the learning curve of those willing and thirsty to learn, and assist the rest to become more efficient learners. Manipulation of data, analyses, forecasting, and data retention will eventually become the domain of nano-computers worn on students' wrists. Students will ask their computer companions questions, or give the parameters of problems, and the master computer will supply the appropriate answers, solutions, options, and choices via their wrist computer companions.

The basic 3Rs will still need to be taught in grade school, and basic overviews given in all fundamental curriculum subjects through middle grades. However, once students have learned the basic relationships and concepts, their computer companions will fill in the gaps, the details, and the facts. Once a child has completed kindergarten through sixth grade, before their thirteenth birthday, they can matriculate to various educational options. They will have already mastered the basics of reading, writing, speech, communication, and arithmetic (few will ever need to know algebra or higher math, and shouldn't be forced to learn it). They should be given appropriate personality and aptitude assessments, then advised of the best options that are most suitable for persons with specific types of profiles. Students, along with their parents and computer companions, should mull over the results of the assessments, then decide on the best educational course a child should take after grade school. As children mature and decide to change their educational objectives, new courses can be plotted with the consent of the learner to revise their educational goals and plans.

The education system is failing because it continues to protect the turf of educationalists, rather than to embrace the pervasiveness of technology and to harness its best applications. Teachers and professors need not fear losing their jobs to on-line education brought directly to students' wristwatch computer companions. Children will continue to require guidance on how to get along with others, how to make sensible decisions, how to stay out of trouble, and how to evolve into positive adults who contribute to improving communities and society. Teachers will be able to teach processes and become mentors. Students, rather than being prisoners of the old school or current pedagogies of regurgitation, wrote memorization, testing, and classroom management techniques will instead become liberated self-actualized learners.

We are losing our children, not because learning is not inherently interesting, but because the school system has made learning boring or too demanding, creating one "winner" for every nine "losers." The public education system turns off nine students for every one who remains tuned in. It's not that our students want to fail, but rather they are failing because our school system fails them. Our school system turns eager and curious minds into self-doubting, fearful, learning avoidant unhappy, angry and emotionally damaged teenagers, who become dysfunctional adults, who raise more dysfunctional children to repeat the cycle again.

America is great, not because of its educational system, but in spite of it. The great strides in knowledge, discovery, and invention have not come as a direct result of compulsory education, but as the consequence of elective learning that was achieved by individuals seeking alternatives to the herding strategy and obstacle course evaluation paradigm of teaching that is prevalent in the educational system. The sure thing our education system consistently achieves is the social conditioning of our children into mindless consumers, whose self-image depends on mass media marketing to define value and worth, where their lives become empty unless they can identify with a brand name, a team, and a changing fad. If that's how our society wants to waste the potential of our youth, by turning them from excited and curious learners to seekers of packaged answers, then woe be to our civilization as we continue to plant our own eventual destruction.

It is not too late to turn things around after generations of failure. But our educational bureaucracy is ingrained with career egotists who feel their intellectual superiority and high-test scores enable them to dictate what's best for our children. These architects of our educational system understand little of what motivates children to learn, and less of what is necessary for children to feel fulfilled and successful. All these curriculum experts know is how to dump more and more facts on minds that will retain less than 5% of everything that is ever taught in school. Instead, students will turn more and more to computer technology to find the answers and facts that they need to succeed in their everyday lives. At the point our children's learning curve from enhanced technology intersects with classroom teaching pedagogies, and their desire for personalized learning exceeds their patience and willingness to attend class, there will be a revolt and an educational revolution. The old ways and current pedagogies will be forced aside, and a new era of individualized learning shall prevail, with or without the participation of educationalists.

If students learn what is personally important to them, while learning about the world, society, and their environment, then they will feel more satisfied and fulfilled with a purposeful education. Let's begin to convince our educationalists and politicians that our society will be vastly improved if we trust our children enough to open the gates to the corrals, and let our children run. Let them experience the exhilaration of moving their own feet to their hearts content, instead of being herded to as mindless followers to the slaughterhouse of a purposeless consumerist life that is devoid of a sense of community or care for the world.

No, it's still not too late to change the educational paradigm. It's just too unlikely. And that's too bad for every child who must endure the feeling of failure and punishment for learning. The ACE demonstration project is proposed to act as our children's last chance to find meaning in an education system that discourages rather than encourages, punishes rather than rewards, and pushes group norms in spite of our children's ingrain need and desire for individual expression and personal discovery. Let the visionaries recognize the simplicity and pragmatic strategies that have been presented by the ACE Proposal. Let those who are blinded by self-interests or egotism, and those who are cynical or fearful of change be ignored, as they have ignored the fundamental flaws and inadequacies of our public education system, with profound damage to our current and future generations of youth. It is not too late to reverse the alienation of our children, and to instill a desire for life long learning and retooling for future careers. We need only to think outside of the traditional box, be willing to explore options, and take action to improve our public schools.

# CHAPTER FIVE – HOMELESSNESS

People from other nations who visit America are often dumbfounded and perplexed as to the reasons why hundreds of thousands of people are homeless in arguably the wealthiest nation in the world. Primarily an urban dilemma, we find an alarming increase in the numbers of children and families among the homeless populations. The reasons vary why people end up living on the streets, in homeless encampments and in public shelters. Among the reasons are extreme poverty and economic plight due to lack of sustainable employment, mental illness, post traumatic syndrome in many veterans returning from warfare, alcoholism, drug addiction, and in some cases personal preference due to a lack of more attractive options available to those who would otherwise prefer a roof over their heads.

As both the temporary and long term effects of the 2009 recessions appears to linger, many families are finding themselves only a paycheck away from homelessness. There were several times when I could have become homeless due to loss of employment for various reasons, and I had to rely on savings, sale of my house for its equity, early withdrawal of retirement funds, running up credit card charges, drastically reducing lifestyle and survival expenses, borrowing from family, temporarily moving in with willing family members, sale of personal property and the safety net of unemployment benefits.  Many others did not have the broad options that I had to implement as their houses may have negative equity, insufficient cash value in their insurance policies, no early withdrawal options in their retirement accounts, or lack of family or close friends willing to help with a shelter from the dangers and challenges of living on the streets.  Many who fall on bad times sometimes turn to crime.  I was lucky I neither became homeless or a criminal... but that wasn't an impossible alternate scenario.

As part of her high school senior civic affairs project, I accompanied my daughter to downtown Los Angeles "skid row" section of town so she could gather photographic documentation of people who were homeless and to attempt to assess why people became destitute.  She developed a survey that she tried to ask homeless persons to determine the reasons for their poverty and homelessness.  Few cooperated as too often the homeless were not prone to answer such personal questions.  I surmise the Department of Social Services employs similar assessment and evaluation tools, but since I never applied for welfare nor did I become homeless, I can only presume.

## HOMELESSNESS QUESTIONNAIRE

First Name:              Age:              Gender:
Ethnic Background:    Legal Marital Status:
Number of Custodial Children:

Number of Non-custodial Children:

Educational Level:

THE PAST:

1. How long have you considered yourself "homeless"?
2. What was your last job before becoming homeless?
3. How long was the period between your last job and becoming homeless?
4. What caused you to stop your employment?
5. What was your income level at the time you became homeless?
6. Why do you think you became homeless?
   Lack of money, loss of employment, illness, alcohol, drugs, etc.?
7. Did you ever think that you could or would become homeless?
8. Who lived with you at the time before you became homeless?
9. Describe the process of losing people from your life as you became homeless. Loss of spouse, children, parents, friends?
10. What was your emotional state in reaction to questions #4 and #6, above?
11. Was there anything you could have done to prevent yourself from becoming homeless?

THE PRESENT:

1. What family members and friends do you still talk to, see, or visit?
2. Where are your "loved ones" nowadays, who you no longer contact?
3. What is the general attitude of your family and friends toward you?
4. What positive things have you experienced in being homeless?
5. What aspects of "living on the streets" do you like?
5. What negative things have you experienced in being homeless?
7. What aspects of living on the streets do you dislike?
8. What do you miss most about your previous life style?
9. If you could change your life now, what are the 5 things you would do first?

THE FUTURE:

1. What are the chances that you will "get back on your feet someday?
2. Who do you think can help you to get going again?
3. What do you think you'll be doing in a year from now?
4. What advice would you give to others who may be facing a similar predicament to what you faced before you became homeless?
5. How can other people avoid becoming homeless?

# CHAPTER SIX - The Socialization of Gender

Society appears as a matrix of illusions and distortions, as the result of the unequal structure of gender roles and values that prevail in all areas of life and at all levels of human interaction. Why are the basically simple ideas of equality, fairness, and justice so fleeting and unattainable in what we perceive as reality? Is it because we have all been socially, culturally, and philosophically conditioned to suppress our true inner selves in order to conform to an artificially imposed structure of reality that primarily benefits the dominant male status quo? What is the truer reality that could, would, and should exist were humans permitted and able to shed the suppressive and oppressive veil of social reality based upon gender inequities? Gender disparity is the foundation of the power dichotomy between the sexes that feeds on injustice to the great benefit of men, and at the greater disadvantage and suffering of the world's women. In a gender free egalitarian society, it would be "normal" for people to...

1.      Dress anyway they want, for their own comfort and self-expression, without being subjected to ridicule, or social penalties for failing to conform to gender norms;

2.      Feel empowered to speak out, to share their feelings and opinions without fear of judgment and ostracism from others for gender-inappropriate views;

3.     Have genuine equal opportunity to pursue career, education, association, and lifestyle, without obstruction or intrusion from government and other groups; and,

4.     Be liberated from concepts such as masculinity, femininity and sexuality, and instead respond to their own personal needs and expressions without fear of punishment for non-conformity.

The barriers to the idealistic egalitarian gender-free society are formidable.  Gender and sex stereotypes continue to be reinforced and enforced through the social and cultural infrastructure of society.  Men continue to maintain a significant advantage in almost all areas of life as compared to women, and gender stereotypes are so pervasive that incremental changes appear to be manifested on a generational level, not as a change to the male power paradigm, but merely as the inclusion of token numbers of females to participate in a power structure designed by men primarily for men.  This paper attempts to measure existing gender stereotypes in a college setting, with the presumption that even among higher educated persons, significant traditional sex and gender stereotypes continue to be perceived as the operative reality.

Survey Methodology and Results

An anonymous sex survey (Appendix A) was randomly distributed to both male and female college students at a multi-racial urban university. The sample consisted of 50 females and 50 males. Responses were tabulated and are reported in Appendix B. Any respondent population under 1000 is usually statistically insignificant, and consequently, based on a small sampling of only 100 students, readers should not generalize any trends that the data may appear to suggest.

Survey Responses – Results

A.      In general (individual variations aside), which sex does better when compared to the other? Please circle one response for each of the following: Answers: 16 female, 34 male, 38      both same, 8 not sure

B.      In general (individual variations aside), which sex does better in each of the following jobs when compared to the other? Please circle one response for each: Answers: Female Jobs: 51 females, 17 males, 25 both same, 7 not sure
Male  jobs:      10 female, 64 male, 15 both same, 11 not sure

C.    In general (individual variations aside), which sex is a better driver/rider of the following types of vehicles when compared to the other?  Please circle one response:
Results: 7 female, 60 male, 24 both same, 9 I'm not sure


D.    Persons of which sex are more likely to have same-sex intimacy (sexual intercourse)?
12  female       17  male       59  both same       12  I'm not sure


E.    The statement, "Size does matter" would best describe the concerns of which sex?
14  females      21  males      31  both same      34  I'm not sure


F.    Which couple do you feel most average people would feel looks odd or weird?
91  short male with tall female        1   short female with tall male
3  short male with tall male     3   short female with tall female


G.    Body and facial hair looks best on persons of which sex?
0   female       96  male       0   both same       4  I'm not sure


H.    Persons of which sex are more likely to commit violent crimes?
3   female       75  male       9   both same       13  I'm not sure


I.    Regarding your answer in the previous question, do you feel violence is mostly due to:
23   heredity     31  environment    13  culture     30  media

J.      Should females be permitted to fight in hand to hand combat in the battlefields?

8   yes         62  no         30  I'm not sure


K.      Should females be allowed to control the buttons that launches nuclear missiles?

21  yes         37  no             42  I'm not sure


L.      Is it the primary role of men in society to protect women?

59  yes         11  no             30  I'm not sure


M.      Is it okay for women to wear pants to any type of job, even if it calls for skirts?

52  yes         21  no             27  I'm not sure


N.      Is it okay for men to wear skirts or dresses in public or in the workplace?

7   yes  66  no             27  I'm not sure


O.      In general, would you agree that most women belong to the weaker gender?   59   yes     17  no         24  I'm not sure


P.      Would you approve your lover having extra-relational sex if their partner were of the same biological sex?

25 yes, 51 no, 24 I'm not sure


Q.      If you were born again in the present time, which sex would you want to be?   39  female     47  male     8  both same

6 I'm not sure

The data suggested that many of the male strength, macho, aggression and protection stereotypes remain intact. Females continue to be relegated only secondarily to men, and are generally viewed as the weaker sex, but with more social freedoms than men. Certain gendered social norms are apparent, relating to facial and body hair, clothing options, and perception of violent tendencies. On the measures of career opportunity and options, it appears that respondents recognize that traditionally masculine types of jobs continue to favor men, while women are type cast into lower paying human service jobs where patience is virtue over power.

## Scholars' Views

Much has been written about gender roles and the divergent social value associated with each sex, leading to the reinforcement of unequal gender roles, expectation, and stereotypes throughout the lives of females. Beginning at birth, parents from high versus low status demonstrate gender preferences that tend to benefit males. Trivers and Willard argue that historically, low-ranking parents have produced the greatest number of grandchildren by investing more in their daughters than their sons, while high-ranking parents achieved the most progeny by investing in sons over daughters. Also, the tendency for parents across all social strata to save more for the college education of their sons than daughters is typical since the expected economic returns are higher for males than for females (Freese & Powell, 1999). Even when women are able to compete "in a man's world", Blair (1999) reports that women have few female role models and believe that their career paths are unpredictable and marked by flukes and accidents.

Furthermore, women face contradictory paradigms for structuring their lives. For example, the male managerial cultural pattern of intense commitment to the organization during the first several years of the career ladder coincides with the life-cycle point at which women are having children. Also in cases where firms disallow married couples to work in the same department, it is generally assumed that the woman rather than her husband would leave due to his typically higher and steadier career path opportunities and income. Even when executive women have prestigious, highly paid jobs, they compare themselves and try to assimilate to the predominantly male management culture, and thus their male dominated financial organizations have been virtually unaffected by feminist concerns (Blair, 1999). Gender inequities show up even at the end of careers, as Han and Moen (1999) observed that gender appears to play an important role in the planning, expectation, and scheduling of retirement, where men are more likely to plan for retirement and to actually retire earlier than women due to the gendered nature of life and career pathways (Han & Moen, 1999).

Gender inequalities "from the cradle to the grave" have been a broad and resistant challenge to the feminist agenda. According to Manza and Brooks (1998), women voters tend to support a wide range of "materialist" social policies such as protective wage and hours laws, expansive health and housing policies, and social provision for homeless women and families, and therefore tend to vote for more expanded social spending by Democrats (Manza & Brooks, 1998). Even so, most men tend to support national defense budget escalations that are usually part of the Republican agenda to reward the military-industrial complex. The hundreds of billions of dollars spent annually on military hardware, international policing functions, foreign and now domestic battlefronts far exceeds that spent on issues that concern feminist causes, besides education.

Meanwhile, mass media continues its daily blitz by depicting females in traditional gender roles, objectifying them for commercial exploitation, and victimizing them as program entertainment. Even where heroines have starring roles, they tend to have an entire supporting cast where they find emotional and physical support and comfort. Buffy the Vampire Slayer, and Zena the Warrior Princess are indicative of the new tougher female characters; however, they are not like Superman, and the Gladiator, who were powerful men who fought alone, and stood on their own feet, without the support of others.

# Discussion

The foundation of "isms" lie in the dichotomous power relationship between male and females, where males have parlayed superior upper body strength and aggressiveness into the global institutions of sexism, racism, and elitism. Beginning at birth, males by their "birthright" are placed in a superior position to their mothers, sisters, aunts, grandmothers, and eventually their wives. Almost universally, societies and cultures espouse male dominance and the male agenda, as exploiter and oppressor of females. Men become blind to the basic contradiction that the females who gave them life, affection, guidance, and nurturance are then castigated into lives of submission, exploitation and violence from men. Civilizations record "his" story, as representative of the greatness of male progress, where females and other disempowered classes receive little or no recognition for their significant contributions and interventions.

The pursuit of masculine values and benefits have created a severe distortion of the potential for world peace and advancement by focusing natural and human resources primarily on military and monetary acquisitions, resulting in wars and plundering. Power and leadership has almost always resided with males (even where a few females have been the heads of states, they occupied such high positions only through the support of the male-controlled military).

Consequently, societies and cultures have generally neglected or devalued those traits typically attributed to femininity and feminism, while praising masculine traits and orientation.

A comparison of prescribed masculine values to feminine values exposes the fundamental contradiction and hypocrisy that has become endemic to the world's social order. The male paradigm emphasizes characteristics that are generally valued as worldly strengths, while the female paradigm is viewed as domestic, sensitive, and weak. Masculine strengths and focus are emphasized in the lexicon of maleness, including competitiveness, winning (at any cost), exploration, discovery, decisiveness, conquering, prevailing, defeating, aggression, leading, persisting, resisting, rebelling, power, control, killing, and war. A perspective of weakness, submission, nurturance, emotionality, obedience, dependence, confusion, security, fear, and domestication generally undervalues females.

The man's worldview, preoccupation, and reach is viewed as a global orientation, while the woman's perspective is seen as domestic or regional, or less than the broader scope of men. Let's take a closer look at what the male dominance paradigm has brought to our planet, and ask if traditional feminine attributions might have brought more progress and peace to our world. In our "man's world", humans have experienced violence, war, serfdom, colonialism, slavery, torture, rape, genocide, disorder, starvation, the atomic bomb, and other weapons of mass destruction, while the Earth has undergone mass species extinctions and environmental pollution as the direct consequence of the masculine agenda of greed and conquest. In contrast, the female role and contributions have included birth, rebirth, regeneration, nurturance, cleanliness, social order, communication, cooperation, maintenance, education of the young, peace, and security.

Which does our world need more, the outcomes of the male paradigm that almost invariably leads to warfare, or the female paradigm that leads to birth and regeneration? Presuming a majority of men will philosophically ascribe to regeneration in preference to war and mayhem, what is wrong with the world system that blocks humans from attaining peace, security, and regeneration that the female paradigm represents? What prejudices persist that continue to affront and block the humanitarian evolution of the human species? Or are we to presume that the underlying factor that has steered the course of human events has been men's biochemical brain chemistry responding to heightened levels of testosterone? Why men are consistently more likely to be violent as compared to women is likely an interaction and product of different brain chemistry and socialization that gives men the feeling and expectation of power, and females the feeling of helplessness, fear and victimization.

## Conclusions

It is clear that unless fundamental changes are made to the male paradigm, females will continue to suffer the disadvantages of finding definition in comparison to men. As women's socialization emphasizes their attractiveness and value to men, males are also conditioned to project masculine behaviors to other men. There appears to exist three areas where men exert the most effort to validate themselves before other men, and attempt to build a consistent self-image of masculinity. These three primary areas of masculine validation and reinforcement are 1) masculine occupation, 2) masculine dominance over females, and 3) masculine attitude and behavior.

Men need to feel important and valued. Their high ego needs reflect their constant need to overcome deep-rooted insecurities that of needing to appear, feel, and behave differently from females, which continues to be a devalued paradigm in almost all human societies. The pursuit of significance and superiority over females causes men to define their self-identity and sense of self-worth according to their occupation, male-typical behaviors, and dominance over women. Primary indicators of being a "winner" and not a "loser" involves a prestigious job title, income level, degree of supervisory authority, professional designation and independence, physical strength, stamina and skills (blue collar paradigm), and admiration or credit for personal achievements.

Contributing to this drive for manhood is the need to downgrade females as a primary socialization strategy to enforce masculine dominance and valuation. In relationships with women, men express the desire of ownership, dominance and control, and view their objectified female counterparts as sex objects whose role is to comfort and serve male desires and needs. Naturally, this male gaze reinforces their role as the protector of their sexual property, women.

Thirdly, the daily reinvention and reiteration of masculine attitudes and behaviors subjects men to a myriad of prescriptions to prove and validate their manhood to their peers, both male and female. Among these are complex processes and expectations that challenge and stress masculinity as requisites to validate masculine self-worth. "Normal" manly attitudes and behavioral expectations include:

1. Possessive of personal property
2. Possessive of females
3. Protective of females and children
4. Anti-gay and anti-wimp orientation
5. Objectification of females
6. High interest in viewing men sports competitions
7. Sports participation and competent skills
8. Beer drinking "with the guys"
9. Minimal amount of occasional drug indulgence
10. Ability and willingness to fight other guys
11. Mentality for aggression, both verbal and physical

12. Interest and competence in "guy things"

13. Ability to withstand pain without crying, just "sucking it in"

14. Not crying in public, except in an acceptable situation (funeral)

15. Desire to take revenge when wronged by others

16. Rebelling and not cooperating with authority

17. Being independent and uncontrollable

18. Risk taking and dangerous behaviors

19. Doing stupid, ridiculous and risky things to impress others

20. Clowning around, joking, teasing, and sexual harassment

21. Talking to others about external, non-disclosing issues

22. Insistence on obtaining "respect" from others

23. Owning male symbols, such as manly vehicles

24. Wearing male validating clothing, and not feminine styles

25. Not giving up, persistence, and winning at all costs

26. Being physically and sexually attractive to females

27. Ability, desire, or willingness to fight and kill others

28. Affinity for destruction, breaking things and blowing things up

29. Exhibiting bravery and courage and not cowardice

30. Possessing sexual stamina with females

Being a "man" is not an easy task. The lengthy list of criteria places enormous pressure on men to "front" their socialized idea of masculinity to other men, and to women who supposedly (and in too many cases) expect the "entire package" of masculine traits and behaviors. Were a man to demonstrate violations of any of the expected manly behavioral traits, then his manhood is put in question by others, which makes him insecure, and consequently causes him to correct his deviation from the masculine norms, in order to validate his self-worth as a man to himself and to the world of men, and to those women who have bought into masculine gender stereotyping. So much needs to be done to free women from male dominance, exploitation, control, and abuse, but in tandem with female liberation will be the freeing of men from the oppressive male paradigm. Consequently, liberating females from their gender roles serves to free men from the culture of manhood, and all the commensurate, unrealistic, and negative attributes that accompany the masculine paradigm.

Men feel validated by feelings from experiences when facing danger and potential death. Even shy boys, who in the course of growing up are bullied, attempt to overcome childhood emasculation by facing danger, fear, ridicule and prejudice. It is not uncommon in certain parts of rough neighborhoods for boys to be stabbed, beat up, robbed at gun point and have to endure many painful incidents of physical and verbal abuse and violence. Yet they usually survive, only to seek peace and freedom away from violent environments.

Fear and victimization causes life-long trauma and that results in deep-rooted anxieties. I can still feel my skin "tingle" when I enter a "bad neighborhood", and I instantly become more "on guard" and aware of my surroundings. I become more observant of people around me, to ascertain their potential threat level. I avoid certain types of streets, alleys, dead ends, and stay on major thoroughfares, take care of business, then leave as soon as possible. I'm not stupid enough to be caught walking down the street in racial and ethnic enclaves in disadvantaged areas where I would stand out from the crowd. I'm not scared, just experienced and cautious. My observations are well grounded in the reality of street life, as teenage offenders who I teach in juvenile detention camp and alternative school settings confirm it on a regular basis. I have a very intimate understanding of violence, and paroled young adults have described the terrible racial conflict that exists behind the walls of state penitentiaries.

Another consequence of post-traumatic stress is to take proactive steps to increase one's confidence, when avoiding dangerous situations fail to bring security. Self-defense strategy is one very positive program to restore or prepare women, girls and shy boys to feel more self-confident and empowered. Since nice people can't always avoid jerks and predators, and can't talk them down from aggressive posturing, then they must be prepared to fight them with every ounce of strength in their bodies and minds. It would be much better to get beat up or killed after "trying", rather than "crying" and allowing attackers to be unscathed and uninjured. It's better to teach an attacker the life lesson that they also stand a chance of great bodily harm, or even possible death, than to let them feel that they can victimize others with impunity.

Bullies and violent predatory criminals have no respect, except in the face of a formidable counterforce. The bottom line is a mind set, that if someone has to die at a given moment in time, let it be the one who is the evil one, the predatory attacker. Our community and society needs more people who contribute positively to the world, and the world would be better off for each perverted violent predator who vanishes from the face of the earth.

The deliberate and premeditated victimization of females has been "his" story. Being victimized by a male dominated and controlled hierarchical world social order has been "her" story. We urgently need to press onward to remove the "his" from the story. We need to develop a world that tells an honest story, across ethnic, cultural, sex and gender distinctions. Everyone in the world is uniquely complex and rich with experiences, abilities, skills, and feelings, all yearning to be expressed, accepted, and praised.

Unfortunately, the world is a matrix of lies and illusions, as the result of the unequal structure of sex, gender roles and values that prevail in all areas of life and at all levels of human interaction. Why are the basically simple ideas of equality, fairness, and justice so fleeting and unattainable in what we perceive as reality? Is it because we have all been socially, culturally, and philosophically conditioned to suppress our true inner selves in order to conform to an artificially imposed structure of reality that primarily benefits the dominant male status quo?

What is the truer reality that could, would, and should exist were humans permitted and able (if possible) to shed the suppressive and oppressive veil of social reality based upon gender inequities? Gender disparity is the foundation of the power dichotomy between the sexes that feeds on injustice to the great benefit of men at the greater disadvantage and suffering of the world's women.

If sexism and gender dichotomy didn't exist, each human being would be free to pursue their own personal development in ways that benefit themselves, without feeling the desire to subjugate and exploit others. True freedom of expression from every aspect of one's inner directed being would be possible, resulting in a world where people deal with events, and relate to each other in an acceptable manner, founded squarely in a true reality, and not an artificially imposed illusion of reality based upon social hierarchy and exploitation. Why can't we have a world where:

1. People can dress anyway they want, for their own comfort and self-expression, without being subjected to ridicule, or social penalties for failing to conform to fads and social norms?

2. People feel intimidated to speak out, to share their feelings and opinions without fear of judgment and ostracism from others, where political correctness does not exist as a concept?

3. People have genuine equal opportunity to pursue career, education, association, and lifestyle, without obstruction or intrusion from parents, government and other groups?

4. Each child born has an unalienable right to adequate love, food, shelter, education, safety, and security, and is liberated from the fear of uncertainty?

5. People are encouraged to help others, to have ample opportunities to learn the arts, music, literature, theatre, and other cultural diversities, and to enrich their lives and the human spirit?

6. Each individual is liberated from concepts such as masculinity, femininity, and sexuality, and instead respond to their own personal needs and expressions without fear of punishment for non-conformity, as long as others are not hurt?

7. The concepts of race, gender, class, correctness, power, hierarchy, and monetary wealth do not exist, but instead each person is viewed and valued as a uniquely gifted, self-empowered and contributing member to the community of Homo sapiens?

Now, which reality would most people prefer to live in... the current highly structured illusions that we call reality, or the reality that could exist, if people let it happen? How is the educational system and mass media being responsible in helping people to gain meaningful insights and enlightenment? How can our social institutions give food for thought to present optional worldview to the reality that exist, and ones that might be possible under a different world paradigm?

The pursuit of masculine values and benefits have created a severe distortion of the potential for world peace and advancement by focusing natural and human resources primarily on military and monetary acquisitions, resulting in wars and plundering. Power and leadership has almost always resided with males (even where a few females have been the heads of states, they occupied such high positions only through the support of the male-controlled military). Consequently, societies and cultures have generally neglected or devalued those traits typically attributed to femininity and feminism, while praising masculine traits and orientation.

A comparison of prescribed masculine values to feminine values exposes the fundamental contradiction and hypocrisy that has become endemic to the world's social order. The male paradigm emphasize characteristics that are generally valued as worldly strengths, while the female paradigm is viewed as domestic, sensitive, and weak. Masculine strengths and focus are emphasized in the lexicon of maleness, including competitiveness, winning (at any cost), exploration, discovery, decisiveness, conquering, prevailing, defeating, aggression, leading, persisting, resisting, rebelling, power, control, killing, and war. A perspective of weakness, submission, nurturance, emotionality, obedience, dependence, confusion, security, fear, and domestication generally undervalues females.

The man's worldview, preoccupation, and reach is viewed as a global orientation, while the woman's perspective is seen as domestic or regional, or less than the broader scope of men. Let's take a closer look at what the male dominance paradigm has brought to our planet, and ask if traditional feminine attributions might have brought more progress and peace to our world. In our "man's world", humans have experienced violence, war, serfdom, colonialism, slavery, torture, rape, genocide, disorder, starvation, the atomic bomb, and other weapons of mass destruction, while the Earth has undergone mass species extinctions as the direct consequence of the masculine agenda of greed and conquest. In contrast, the female role and contributions have included birth, rebirth, regeneration, nurturance, cleanliness, social order, communication, cooperation, maintenance, education of the young, peace, and security.

Which does our world need more, the outcomes of the male paradigm that almost invariably leads to warfare, or the female paradigm that leads to birth and regeneration? Presuming a majority of men will philosophically ascribe to regeneration in preference to war and mayhem, what is wrong with the world system that blocks humans from attaining peace, security, and regeneration that the female paradigm represents? What prejudices persist that continue to affront and block the humanitarian evolution of the human species? Or are we to presume that the underlying factor that has steered the course of human events has been biochemical brain chemistry responding to heightened levels of testosterone?

Almost all women have to go through negative experiences with men sometime during their lives. Meeting men who appear to be fun, normal, and relatively intelligent is no guarantee they may have met the psycho from hell. Borderline psychotics are attracted to open, kind and vulnerable persons who appear to be defenseless victim types. So-called "friends" become unhappily rejected stalkers whose potentially violent tendencies result in two possible futures, death or the penitentiary.

Statistics indicate that ten percent of the general population has the propensity for great violence, and it's the men in this group that poses the greatest danger to the public, especially to women, because they comprise society's typical predators. Of course, there's also the neighbor next door, the co-worker, the family member, the date, all of whom pose even greater danger because a woman's guard would be down around men they think they can trust.

Statistics also indicate that women stand up to a ten-fold increase of assault, rape, or violence from someone who they know than from a stranger, but the terror is greatest when attacked by strangers because familiarity seems to decrease fear, while increasing anger from victims due to the feeling that their trust was violated. Attacks by strangers involve an animalistic level of fear due to surprise and uncertainty.

Why men are 10 times more likely to be violent as compared to women is likely an interaction and product of different brain chemistry and socialization that gives men the feeling and expectation of power, and females the feeling of helplessness, fear and victimization. The foundation of "isms" lie in the dichotomous power relationship between male and females, where males have parlayed superior upper body strength and aggressiveness into the global institutions of sexism, racism, and elitism. Beginning at birth, males by their "birthright" are placed in a superior position to their mothers, sisters, aunts, grandmothers, and eventually their wives. Almost universally, societies and cultures espouse male dominance and the male agenda, as exploiter and oppressor of females. Men become blind to the basic contradiction that the females who gave them life, affection, guidance, and nurturance are then castigated into lives of submission, exploitation and violence from men. Civilizations record "his" story, as the truthful representative of the greatness of male progress, where females and other disempowered classes receive little or no recognition for their significant contributions and interventions.

Solutions and Recommendations

In order to empower themselves against aggressors, less physically powerful people, especially women, need to learn alternatives to fight victimization in the form of physical, emotional, and mental self-defense:

1. Physical Defense Strategy: A maximum strategy for maximum danger, or paranoia. A lesser continuum as justified by a higher security level of the immediate environment. These steps are suggested to improve a female chances, when alone, to repel an attack by a determined predatory attacker, and to survive.

   a. Learn practical self-defense techniques, both weaponless, and with various weapons that can be readily found in the environment, like a sharp car key, belt, sharp pen, purse strap, pump heels, rocks, forks, spoons, pots and pans, furniture, lamps, fire extinguisher, and whatever is near by during an attack. Basic self-defense includes using an attacker's weight and momentum against him, and using the hard surfaces from one's body (elbow, fist, hand ridge, knees, head, heel, etc.) against the soft surfaces of the attacker (testicles, throat, eyes, ears, etc.). Full contact self defense training is essential to provide a realistic experience in how it feels to strike an attacker with full force.

   b. Carry legal self-defense weapons, like pepper spray or a stun gun, ready for use when in an uncomfortable or potentially foreboding environment. A blinding halogen flashlight is also helpful during nighttime attacks. Be familiar with its use, and never carry a weapon that can be taken away and used for deadly harm against the potential victim.

c.   Learn to use a firearm, knife, pipe, stick, and other objects that can be stored in handy places somewhere in each room, near where women are more likely to spend more time.  Depending upon the safety of one's neighborhood, there should be at least one object that can be used as a self-defense weapon in each room of one's house, hidden, and known only to the resident.  However, care should be used if there are small or immature minors at home.  For example:

1)   Bedroom door is alarmed, minimally with a trip alarm that sounds a high decibel screech.  Objects are strategically tied to curtains and blinds next to windows, which will fall over with great noise if an intruder enters, to supplement an electronic window alarms system.  Pepper spray should be placed on the bed stand next to one's clock, safety off, to be reachable.  A loaded small caliber gun, cocked and with safety on (and trigger locked if minors reside in home) should be placed

beneath the bed, so if attacked, the woman can fall to the floor and have a chance to grab and use the gun (the gun is unlocked and ready for use after retiring to bedroom to sleep). The smaller caliber gun (.22 caliber) may not kill a large male, but gives the woman a chance to get up and run to the place where her larger caliber weapon is ready for use. According to the NRA, at least 200,000 incidents per year of gun-related home defense occur annually, compared to 8,000 homicides on a national basis. There should also be sharp hairpins and letter openers handily on the dresser, near the makeup vanity, and also taped to the bottom of the sitting chair. Bedroom doors and locks should be strong, with key access, to keep out a large charging man.

2) Bathroom: take your loaded gun with you into the shower or bath, but try not to drop it into the soapy water (but it'll still work when wet). The handle of the bathroom plunger should be sharpened (and a metal cross bow arrow tip installed), and

covered with a plastic cap that can be easily removed, and used a thrusting weapon to the surprise of any attacker. Toothbrushes can also be sharpened and capped off. Tape a 2 inch knife   to the bottom of the sink, and place one in the medicine cabinet, and also placed in the hollow shower curtain tube, and inside towel rack hangers. The bathroom door should be strong, with strong key-accessible deadbolt, and you should have your cell phone handy.

3)     Kitchen: hide and lock all large knives when not being used. Place sharp 2-inch knives (blade length) in several Places (in a few pots, in the dirt of a potted plant, under the chopping board, taped to the side of the range, under or on tope of a shelf, etc.). The small knife is enough to cause pain to an attacker, to allow the female to run to the bedroom for the phone and backup firearm. Leaving large knives around enables burglars to arm themselves, and if taken away from the woman, used against her by a stronger

upper body man, with a stronger grip and greater aggression.

4) Living Room and Den: pepper spray taped to the T.V. remote control (placed out of reach if very small children are around, when not being used with T.V.). Older children should be taught how to use it. Small 2-inch blade knives strategically taped to the bottom of tables and chairs where the woman is most likely to be sitting if an intruder were to break in. Everything must be out of the reach of small children, and older children must be warned and taught on its proper use, only during incident of attack, and not on each other. Children who fight should be kept away from any weapons of any type, as they are too unpredictable and may use it against each other.

5) Garage: a peep hole to the garage from the adjoining interior door should provide a view of the entire garage when lit up. A motion detector alarm system should be

armed.  Some intruders have access to universal garage openers that can open your garage door.  When driving in to the garage, look in the rear view mirror as pulling in, to make sure no one has followed you in. If so, back the car out, and if the intruder is stupid enough to stand behind your car, slowly nudge him out of the way, but don't panic and deliberately run him down... you may kill him. Of course, if he has a gun, duck down, step on the gas, and back the car out quickly to leave the scene.  If the gun-toting intruder is hit, then he had it coming.  At least you're more likely to escape and live.

6)  At work, universally, all employers ban weapons in the work place.  However, women also have the right against illegal search and seizure from their private property, their purses.  Pepper spray hooked to your key ring, another in the purse, tough finger nail files, letter openers, an electronic stun gun, and two inch blade knife would likely be legal.  Carry one, or all, depending on a

woman's level of anxiety and concern.

7) Parking lots and parking structures are potentially dangerous places, especially in certain neighborhoods, particularly after dark when fewer people are around, because predators are opportunistic attackers. The key-ring pepper spray and sharp finger nail file can buy time for the female to scream "fire", "help me", which gets more attention than just screaming. If an attacker is able to get a woman into a vehicle, there's a very high probability she will be raped, tortured, and/or murdered, possibly never to be found again. It is much better for a woman to fall to the ground, and continue to scream and fight, than to cooperate and enter a vehicle. Predators don't want to work all that hard to get a victim, and the more a woman fights in a public area, the less she will have to fight in a remote environment, like an alley, in the forest, desert, or deserted building. It's more likely a predatory attacker will give up and wait for a chance later at a much easier target.

2.      There are also incidents where a single predatory attacker is much too big and strong to be hurt by a smaller person.  Some men can take a hard kick to the testicles, direct strike to their throat, or a jab to the eyes, and still manage to get their strong hands and body on the intended victim.  Ideally, a victim is able to keep sufficient distance between themselves and the attacker to avoid getting grabbed.  For example, placing a car between a potential attacker is a prudent strategy, by going to unlock the door that places the car between a potential attacker and victim.  Running around the car to avoid capture while screaming will also frustrate and discourage most unarmed attackers.  Always keep a large sharpened screwdriver hidden in the car's trunk, and learn how to pop open the trunk if placed inside by an attacker.  The "club" also makes a handy striking weapon, but it can be taken away if a person doesn't know how to use it properly in close fighting quarters.

3.      Mental and emotional strategies are as important, or even more important than physical abilities.  Multiple attackers, armed predators (with guns or knives) cancel most chances of using self-defense techniques or non-lethal weapons (unless the victim already has a loaded gun, cocked, safety off, trigger lock off, and ready to aim and fire, and the intended victim is a damn good shot, and not afraid or morally against shooting another person in self-defense).   A well-trained fighter (like a Navy Seal or Green Beret) stands a 50%

chance of coming out alive against 3 or more men armed with guns who are willing to use them, when the trained fighter is unarmed. Any average man or woman's chances are much less to nil in this case.

Sometimes, pretending to go along with the attacker's program when they are heavily armed, buys a person time to think of escape strategies. Think escape, not fighting back, or the trigger-happy assailants will most likely shoot the victim. A crazed man with a gun has a very different level of agitation and mind set from those who are not willing to use deadly force. A man with a gun is likely not to have moral questions about shooting someone, if he becomes fearful, excited, agitated, or irritated. Cooperate to buy time, and hope he's a bad shot when the opportunity arises for a quick departure (like jumping out of a moving car going 20 mph or less, but knowing how to fall and roll because hitting the pavement will definitely hurt).

All things being said, being aware of one's environment, listening to one's intuition (and women are known to have a better "sixth sense" than most men), assessing potential danger from the situation and people, keeping open a quick escape route, and using non-lethal armed and non-armed self-defense techniques and weapons when verbal interaction fails, to provide escape is probably an effective strategy to avoid capture, violence, and perhaps death. Use verbal and mental skills to assess and emotionally disarm and calm attackers when captive, and looking for opportunities to buy time to escape is essential if kidnapped, but relatively unharmed. If a woman or man has used all of her/his wit, strength, and self-defense training to escape or incapacitate an attacker, they greatly improve their chance for survival. But nothing in life is guaranteed, so if victims should be killed, at least they go out "fighting for their lives", and not as "road kill".

At times, in the rare situation, that's the best a person can hope for; to be able to deliver a counterforce blow to an evil attacker that puts them out of the business of hurting another person. Maybe the attacker loses an eye to the victim, and at times in life, some people's death serves to prevent many others from dying; which is the case of our brave American fighting forces, both women and men, in many nations around the world. If a person must die, there is no greater honor than having fought one's best fight, in the service of one's loved ones and country, for noble principles such as democracy, freedom, liberty, justice, and the American way of life. In the urban battlefields, each citizen has a responsibility to show courage, and to come to the calling of fellow citizens against evil, as long as the actions taken are proper and allowed under the rule of law and good Samaritans, and are not acts of vigilantism. A potential victim has to do what they gotta do, especially if faced with overpowering danger from predatory males who seek females, the young, and the defenseless as their next victims.

# Appendix I

Anonymous Gender Information Survey:  This survey is a class assignment.

A.  In general (individual variations aside), which sex does better when compared to the other?  Please circle one response for each of the following:

1.  Physical strength   a.  female   b.  male   c.  both same
                         d.  I'm not sure

2.  Mental reasoning     a.  female     b.  male   c.  both same
                         d.  I'm not sure

3.  Emotional stability  a.  female     b.  male   c.  both same
                         d.  I'm not sure

4.  Sports performance   a.  female     b.  male   c.  both same
                         d.  I'm not sure

5.  Career positions     a.  female     b.  male   c.  both same
                         d.  I'm not sure

6.  Job salaries         a.  female     b.  male   c.  both same
                         d.  I'm not sure

7.  Rights, and liberties  a.  female   b.  male   c.  both same
                         d.  I'm not sure

8.  Legal protection     a.  female     b.  male   c.  both same
                         d.  I'm not sure

9.  Sexual performance   a.  female     b.  male   c.  both same
                         d.  I'm not sure

10.  Independence & power  a.  female   b.  male   c.  both same
                         d.  I'm not sure

B.  In general (individual variations aside), which sex does better in each of the following jobs when compared to the other?    Please circle one response for each:

1.  Firefighter          a.  female    b. male    c.  both same
                         d.  not sure
2.  Nurse                a.  female    b. male    c.  both same
                         d.  not sure
3.  Doctor               a.  female    b. male    c.  both same
                         d.  not sure
4.  Business executive   a.  female    b. male    c.  both same
                         d.  I'm not sure
5.  Banking executive    a.  female    b. male    c.  both same
                         d.  I'm not sure
6.  Bank teller          a.  female    b. male    c.  both same
                         d.  I'm not sure
7.  Preschool Teacher    a.  female    b. male    c.  both same
                         d.  I'm not sure
8.  Big rig truck driver a.  female    b. male    c.  both same
                         d.  I'm not sure
9.  Nurturing parent     a.  female    b. male    c.  both same
                         d.  I'm not sure
10. Prostitute           a.  female    b. male    c.  both same
                         d.  I'm not sure
11. Military jet pilot    a.  female    b. male    c.  both same
                         d.  I'm not sure

C.   In general (individual variations aside), which sex is a better driver/rider of the following types of vehicles when compared to the other?   Please circle one response:

1.   SUVs                    a.  female    b.  male    c.  both same
                             d.  I'm not sure
2.   Pick-up trucks          a.  female    b.  male    c.  both same
                             d.  I'm not sure
3.   Off-road vehicles       a.  female    b.  male    c.  both same
                             d.  I'm not sure
4.   Motorcycles             a.  female    b.  male    c.  both same
                             d.  I'm not sure
5.   Race cars               a.  female    b.  male    c.  both same
                             d.  I'm not sure
6.   Camper-RV Buses         a.  female    b.  male    c.  both same
                             d.  I'm not sure
7.   Speed boat              a.  female    b.  male    c.  both same
                             d.  I'm not sure
8.   Farm tractor            a.  female    b.  male    c.  both same
                             d.  I'm not sure
9.   Bulldozer               a.  female    b.  male    c.  both same
                             d.  I'm not sure
10.  Military tank           a.  female    b.  male    c.  both same
                             d.  I'm not sure

D.   Persons of which sex are more likely to have same-sex intimacy (sexual intercourse)?
     a.  female    b.  male    c.  both same    d.  I'm not sure

E.	The statement, "Size does matter" would best describe the concerns of which sex?

a. females	b. males	c. both same	d. I'm not sure

F.	Which couple do you feel most average people would feel looks odd or weird?

a. short male with tall female	b. short female with tall male
c. short male with tall male	d. short female with tall female

G.	Body and facial hair looks best on persons of which sex?

a. female	b. male	c. both same	d. I'm not sure

H.	Persons of which sex are more likely to commit violent crimes?

a. female	b. male	c. both same	d. I'm not sure

I.	Regarding your answer in the previous question, do you feel violence is mostly due to:

a. heredity	b. environment	c. culture	d. media

J.	Should females be permitted to fight in hand to hand combat in the battlefields?

a. yes	b. no	c. I'm not sure

K.	Should females be allowed to control the buttons that launches nuclear missiles?

a. yes	b. no	c. I'm not sure

L.  Is it the primary role of men in society to protect women?

   a. yes           b. no          c. I'm not sure


M.  Is it okay for women to wear pants to any type of job, even if it calls for skirts?

   a. yes           b. no          c. I'm not sure


N.  Is it okay for men to wear skirts or dresses in public or in the workplace?

   a. yes           b. no          c. I'm not sure


O.  In general, would you agree that most women belong to the weaker gender?

   a. yes           b. no          c. I'm not sure


P.  Would you approve your lover having extra-relational sex if their partner were of the same biological sex?

   a. yes           b. no          c. I'm not sure


Q.  If you were born again in the present time, which sex would you want to be?

   a. female    b. male    c. both same    d. I'm not sure

Please circle your sex     a. female    b. male

Your sexual preference     a. straight    b.. gay

                       c. lesbian    d. "bi"    e. none

Please circle your age range     a. 18-24    b. 25-34

                       c. 35-44   d. 45 and above

Please circle your education     a. HS grad    b. College

                       c. Advanced degree

## Appendix II: Survey Responses

Anonymous Sex Information Survey

A.     In general (individual variations aside), which sex does better when compared to the other? Please circle one response for each of the following:

1.    Physical strength     7 female    72 male    11 both same
                                 10 I'm not sure

2.    Mental reasoning     13 female    27 male    53 both same
                                 7 I'm not sure

3.    Emotional stability     17 female    21 male    57 both same
                                 5 I'm not sure

4.    Sports performance     13 female    46 male    33 both same
                                 8 I'm not sure

5.    Career positions     12 female    27 male    45 both same
                                 16 I'm not sure

6.    Job salaries     15 female    29 male    41 both same
                                 15 I'm not sure

| 7. | Rights, and liberties | 37 female | 26 male | 38 both same |
| | | 9 I'm not sure | | |
| 8. | Legal protection | 41 female | 19 male | 35 both same |
| | | 5 I'm not sure | | |
| 9. | Sexual performance | 37 female | 26 male | 32 both same |
| | | 5 I'm not sure | | |
| 10. | Public Speaking | 16 female | 47 male | 36 both same |
| | | 7 I'm not sure | | |
| | Average | 16 female | 34 male | 38 both | 8 not sure |

B. In general (individual variations aside), which sex does better in each of the following jobs when compared to the other?    Please circle one response for each:

| 1. | Firefighter | M | 5 female | 75 male |
| | | 12 both same | 12 Not sure | |
| 2. | Nurse | F | 73 female | 13 male |
| | | 4 both same | 4 Not sure | |
| 3. | Doctor | M | 17 female | 64 male |
| | | 6 both same | 6 Not sure | |
| 4. | Corporate executive | M | 13 female | 49 male |
| | | 9 both same | 9 Not sure | |
| 5. | Banking Executive | M | 14 female | 54 male |
| | | 10 both same | 10 Not sure | |
| 6. | Bank teller | F | 37 female | 24 male |
| | | 5 both same | 5 Not sure | |
| 7. | Preschool Teacher | F | 49 female | 19 male |
| | | 5 both same | 5 Not sure | |
| 8. | Big rig truck driver | M | 7 female | 69 male |
| | | 3 both same | 3 Not sure | |

9.       Nurturing parent       F       37 female     15 male  
                                  6   both same    6 Not sure

10.      Prostitute             F       44 female     19 male  
                                  6   both same    6 Not sure

11.      Military Jet Pilot      M       5 female       73 male  
                                  5   both same    5 Not sure

12.      Cosmetic salesperson   F       67 female     9 male  
                                14   both same    14 Not sure

Female Jobs,    Average        51 female     17 male  
                                25   both same    7 Not sure

Male jobs,      Average        10 female     64 male  
                                15   both same    11 Not sure


C.      In general (individual variations aside), which sex is a better driver/rider of the     following types of vehicles when compared to the other?     Please circle one response:


1.      SUVs                   16 female     21 male  
                               57 both same     6 I'm not sure

2.      Pick-up trucks        11 female     42 male  
                               43 both same     4 I'm not sure

3.      Off-road vehicles      7 female      59 male  
                               21 both same     13 I'm not sure

4.      Motorcycles          7 female      62 male  
                               19 both same     12 I'm not sure

5.      Race cars             5 female      73 male  
                               14 both same     8 I'm not sure

6.      Camper-RV Buses    7 female      44 male  
                               26 both same     23 I'm not sure

| 7. | Speed boat | 5 female | 62 male |
| | | 21 both same | 12 I'm not sure |
| 8. | Farm tractor | 3 female | 72 male |
| | | 11 both same | 14 I'm not sure |
| 9. | Bulldozer | 3 female | 77 male |
| | | 11 both same | 9 I'm not sure |
| 10. | Military tank | 4 female | 80 male |
| | | 12 both same | 4 I'm not sure |

Average    7 female      60 male    24 both      9 not sure


D.    Persons of which sex are more likely to have same-sex intimacy (sexual intercourse)?

12  female      17  male      59  both same      12  I'm not sure


E.    The statement, "Size does matter" would best describe the concerns of which sex?

14  females      21  males      31  both same      34  Not sure


F.    Which couple do you feel most average people would feel looks odd or weird?

91  short male with tall female      1  short female with tall male

3  short male with tall male      3  short female with tall female


G.    Body and facial hair looks best on persons of which sex?

0  female      96  male      0  both same      4  I'm not sure

H.    Persons of which sex are more likely to commit violent crimes?

3   female     75  male     9  both same     13  I'm not sure


I.    Regarding your answer in the previous question, do you feel violence is mostly due to:

23   heredity    31  environment    13  culture    30  media


J.    Should females be permitted to fight in hand to hand combat in the battlefields?

8   yes          62  no          30  I'm not sure


K.    Should females be allowed to control the buttons that launches nuclear missiles?

21   yes         37  no                   42  I'm not sure


L.    Is it the primary role of men in society to protect women?

59   yes          11  no       30  I'm not sure


M.    Is it okay for women to wear pants to any type of job, even if it calls for skirts?

52  yes           21  no       27  I'm not sure

N.    Is it okay for men to wear skirts or dresses in public or in the workplace?

7   yes           66  no       27  I'm not sure

O.   In general, would you agree that most women belong to the weaker gender?

59   yes        17  no        24   I'm not sure

P.   Would you approve your lover having extra-relational sex if their partner were of the same biological sex?

25   yes        51  no        24   I'm not sure

Q.   If you were born again in the present time, which sex would you want to be?

39  female     47  male     8  both same     6  I'm not sure


Please circle your sex        50   female      50  male

Your sexual preference        88   straight    3  gay

                              2  lesbian    3  "bi"   4  none

Please circle your age range        71:  18-24     22:  25-34

                                    6:  35-44    1:  45 and above

Please crcle your education         76  HS grad     19  College

                                    5   Advanced degree

# References

Blair-Loy, Mary, 1999. "Career patterns of executive women in finance: all optimal matching analysis." American Journal of Sociology, Vol. 104, Issue 5 (Mar., 1999), 1346-1397. Retrieved from the World Wide Web, March 1, 2002 from http://www.jstor.org.

Freese, Jeremy, and Brian Powell, 1999. "Sociobiology, status, and parental investment in sons and daughters: testing the Trivers-Willard Hypothesis." American Journal of Sociology, Vol. 104, Issue 6 (May, 1999), 1704-1743. Retrieved from the World Wide Web, March 1, 2002 from http://www.jstor.org.

Han, Shin Kap, and Phyllis Moen, 1999. "Clocking out: temporal patterning of retirement." American Journal of Sociology, Vol. 105, Issue 1 (July, 1999), 229-236. Retrieved from the World Wide Web, March 1, 2002 from http://www.jstor.org.

Manza, Jeff, and Clem Brooks, 1998. " The gender gap in U.S. presidential elections; when, why? implications?" American Journal of Sociology, Vol. 103, Issue 5 (Mar., 1998), 1235-1266. Retrieved from the World Wide Web, March 1, 2002 from http://www.jstor.org.

# Chapter Seven –Determining of Race

Racial stereotyping and racist attitudes have long been ascribed to the majoritarian Anglo political culture, which has resulted in a socio-economic dichotomy between whites and persons from other racial groups who live in the United States of America. It's long been the assumption that the victims of racism, whether historical or actual, cannot themselves be racist, and consequently were moderately immune from suspicion of racism based on their skin color. There does not appear to exist much academic research on interracial prejudices among people of color, as racism was defined as the oppression of the minority by the majority, particularly as it reflected hundreds of years of oppressive white on black racial bigotry in America.

As large metropolitan cities became the haven for immigrants, particularly from Latin America, Mexico, and Asia, their rapid population increase and concentrations placed them in direct competition with multi-generational African-American citizens, and each other. Conflict arose from misunderstanding and lack of acceptance or respect among new immigrant groups and those who arrived during earlier eras in the demographics of immigration to the U.S. As groups imported their own indigenous languages, foods, cultures, religions, and worldviews, they found themselves becoming ever more estranged from other ethnic groups in America.

Even among people of similar skin tone (commonly referred to misnomer as "race"), competing for limited jobs on the lower-skilled levels became a routine source of conflict that abetted the adoption of stereotypes already prevalent in the majoritarian culture's political and media definitions of racial minorities. New immigrant groups felt more comfortable huddling together in ethnic enclaves, and consequently reduced the opportunities to interact with residents reflecting other cultures. Indeed, Los Angeles County, and a major metropolitan university such as CSULA are highly diversified, reflecting almost all imaginable shades of skin tone, and hundreds of native heritages, languages, and cultures... mostly passing each other as ships in the night. Los Angeles is rich in human diversity, unfortunately racial stereotypes still persists, as relics of acculturation and misunderstanding.

Methodology

This paper attempts a small random sampling of 110 CSULA students, of which 55 were randomly selected from the University Student Union and Library North, Second Floor, and 55 were students in Dr. Bell's Anthropology 361 class. Surveys were passed out, collected, and responses were tabulated, analyzed, and data patterns were summarized. In the first respondent population, the anonymous survey was passed out in class by the professor, with the instruction that participation was voluntary, and the information was being gathered as part of a classmates project. Papers were left on the professors desk as students left class. In the second respondent group, students were randomly selected from the library and student union, and asked if they would be willing to participate in an anonymous survey for a class. The surveys were left with students, and the investigator returned 15-20 minutes later to retrieve the completed surveys from students, or from tables where they sat while answering survey questions (some completed surveys, then left the area). Surveys were tabulated, and raw scores were summarized. The data was subsequently transformed into a percentage format, and entered into tables categorizing responses and percentage of positive and negative stereotypes.

Survey Results

The raw data tabulations are attached as an appendix to this investigative paper. The following quantitative matrix summarizes the salient results of the surveying instrument. Respondents were asked to check only one answer per question; however, in four instances, 2 boxes were checked, and in two instances, 3 boxes were checked. The data was tabulated and included in the analysis, causing the totals in a few cases to exceed 100 per cent response. Some students did not answer every question on the survey. The data was translated into percentages, based upon total responses divided by the total number of respondents. The percentage data that suggested trends were subjected to statistical analysis for significance, and where none existed, narrative observations were noted.

## Table 1: Survey Responses

Total Number of Respondents = 110

Notes:

Categories are abbreviated from the survey for tabulation efficiency. Data transformed from raw data to percentages for each survey question, rounded to nearest full percent.

1.  What generation do you represent in your family's residence in the U.S.A.?  1st./immigrants = 38% 2nd/born here = 36%  3rd generation = 4% 4th. gen. or greater = 24%

2.  Do you believe that "racism" exist today in America? Yes = 100%  No = 0%

3.  Treated you differently on account of your "race"? Yes = 84%  No = 13%

4. AGE: GENDER: RACE:

| 18-25 | 26-39 | 40-61 | 62+ | M | F |
|---|---|---|---|---|---|
| 58 | 35 | 5 | 0 | 55 | 44 |

| None | Asian | Black | Latin | Native | Other | White |
|---|---|---|---|---|---|---|
| 0 | 13 | 13 | 40 | 3 | 28 | 5 |

5. What do agencies classify your "race"

| None | Asian | Black | Latin | Native | Other | White |
|---|---|---|---|---|---|---|
| 0 | 13 | 13 | 55 | 3 | 12 | 5 |

6. Most likely to complete four-year college degree

| None | Asian | Black | Latin | Native | Other | White |
|---|---|---|---|---|---|---|
| 16 | 25 | 1 | 0 | 0 | 2 | 55 |

7. Most likely to complete a graduate school degree

| None | Asian | Black | Latin | Native | Other | White |
|---|---|---|---|---|---|---|
| 15 | 24 | 0 | 0 | 0 | 3 | 56 |

8. Most likely to "get ahead" at work?

| None | Asian | Black | Latin | Native | Other | White |
|---|---|---|---|---|---|---|
| 6 | 3 | 1 | 1 | 2 | 3 | 81 |

9. Most of the best breaks in life?

| None | Asian | Black | Latin | Native | Other | White |
|---|---|---|---|---|---|---|
| 10 | 4 | 4 | 0 | 1 | 3 | 79 |

10. Most likely to become "unemployed"?

| None | Asian | Black | Latin | Native | Other | White |
|------|-------|-------|-------|--------|-------|-------|
| 13 | 0 | 50 | 21 | 14 | 1 | 2 |

11. Most "intelligent"

| None | Asian | Black | Latin | Native | Other | White |
|------|-------|-------|-------|--------|-------|-------|
| 66 | 23 | 2 | 3 | 0 | 2 | 5 |

12. Most "musically talented"

| None | Asian | Black | Latin | Native | Other | White |
|------|-------|-------|-------|--------|-------|-------|
| 50 | 5 | 25 | 12 | 2 | 2 | 4 |

13. Most "physically talented"

| None | Asian | Black | Latin | Native | Other | White |
|------|-------|-------|-------|--------|-------|-------|
| 40 | 1 | 48 | 3 | 1 | 1 | 5 |

14. Most "inventive" or "innovative"

| None | Asian | Black | Latin | Native | Other | White |
|------|-------|-------|-------|--------|-------|-------|
| 52 | 16 | 5 | 5 | 4 | 3 | 11 |

15. Most "humanitarian"

| None | Asian | Black | Latin | Native | Other | White |
|------|-------|-------|-------|--------|-------|-------|
| 50 | 2 | 5 | 15 | 13 | 2 | 11 |

16. Most "violent"

| None | Asian | Black | Latin | Native | Other | White |
|---|---|---|---|---|---|---|
| 54 | 1 | 15 | 8 | 0 | 1 | 12 |

17. Most "peaceful"

| None | Asian | Black | Latin | Native | Other | White |
|---|---|---|---|---|---|---|
| 47 | 15 | 2 | 2 | 22 | 4 | 6 |

18. Most "best looking"

| None | Asian | Black | Latin | Native | Other | White |
|---|---|---|---|---|---|---|
| 45 | 2 | 9 | 25 | 1 | 5 | 14 |

19. Most "rude" and "inconsiderate"

| None | Asian | Black | Latin | Native | Other | White |
|---|---|---|---|---|---|---|
| 48 | 9 | 23 | 4 | 1 | 3 | 10 |

20. Loudest and wildest

| None | Asian | Black | Latin | Native | Other | White |
|---|---|---|---|---|---|---|
| 42 | 1 | 43 | 4 | 0 | 3 | 6 |

21. Most likely to become alcoholics

| None | Asian | Black | Latin | Native | Other | White |
|---|---|---|---|---|---|---|
| 44 | 1 | 3 | 20 | 15 | 5 | 7 |

22. Most likely to become illegal drug users or drug addicts

| None | Asian | Black | Latin | Native | Other | White |
|------|-------|-------|-------|--------|-------|-------|
| 48   | 2     | 24    | 11    | 2      | 3     | 8     |

23. Most likely to be criminals or be imprisoned

| None | Asian | Black | Latin | Native | Other | White |
|------|-------|-------|-------|--------|-------|-------|
| 39   | 0     | 41    | 12    | 1      | 2     | 5     |

24. Most likely to be homosexual or bi-sexually preferences

| None | Asian | Black | Latin | Native | Other | White |
|------|-------|-------|-------|--------|-------|-------|
| 50   | 1     | 0     | 1     | 0      | 2     | 37    |

25. Most likely to be prejudiced against other races

| None | Asian | Black | Latin | Native | Other | White |
|------|-------|-------|-------|--------|-------|-------|
| 39   | 3     | 7     | 2     | 1      | 2     | 45    |

26. Personal beliefs about the concept of "race"

21% Race is skin color and other physical features that are biologically inherited.

8% Race includes skin color, and other mental or psychological traits.

21% Race is the continent, country, or culture where a person belongs.

38% There is no such thing as "race"; all human beings are of the homo-sapiens species.

10% I'm not sure whether there's such a thing as "race", or not.

27.   Got job on account of "race preference", would you object?        Yes = 54%   No = 38%

28.   If you had the power to eliminate "race" as a "barrier", would you?   Yes = 75%   No = 19%

## Table 2: Distribution of Positive and Negative Stereotypes by Race, Class Respondents
(Ranking highest number [a], and second [b] highest number of responses)

Total Positive Stereotypes

| Number | None | Asian | Black | Latin | Native | Other | White |
|---|---|---|---|---|---|---|---|
| 11 | 6a ,3b | 3b | 1a,1b | 2b | 1b | 0 | 4a,1b |

Total Negative Stereotypes

| Number | None | Asian | Black | Latin | Native | Other | White |
|---|---|---|---|---|---|---|---|
| 9 | 5a ,3b | 1b | 3a,3b | 2b | 0 | 0 | 1a,1b |

Total Stereotypes & Ranking   20

As a Percentage

Total Positive Stereotypes

| Number | None | Asian | Black | Latin | Native | Other | White |
|---|---|---|---|---|---|---|---|
| 55 | 55/27 | 27b | 9/9 | 18b | 9b | 0 | 36/9 |

Total Negative Stereotypes

| Number | None | Asian | Black | Latin | Native | Other | White |
|---|---|---|---|---|---|---|---|
| 45 | 56/33 | 11b | 33/33 | 22b | 0 | 0 | 11/11 |

Total Stereotypes & Ranking     100

By Majoritarian Social-Cultural Stereotypic Generalized "Standards"
Total Positive Stereotypes in Questions #6, 7, 8, 9, 11, 12, 13, 14, 15, 17, 18
Total Negative Stereotypes in Questions #10, 16, 19, 20, 21, 22, 23, 24

## Discussion

The United States has increasingly become a multiethnic society where its laws and other cultural practices have applied ethnic categorization as one of the main bases of social identity and social privilege. Patriotism was also used as a way to identify whites at a higher ethnic level, and to assign lower levels to ethnic minorities. Especially in the South, patriotism among whites was associated with classical racism, social dominance orientation, and opposition to interracial marriage, while patriotism with ethnic minorities (particularly African-Americans) usually suggested the exact opposite attitudes. In the case of African Americans, all U.S. history texts address the issue of slavery, discrimination, and the denial of civil rights; but little attention is focused on African American intellectual, economic, and technological achievements or on the past and present contributions of blacks to the development of the United States. This absence of accurate historical data on the contributions of minorities lend students to believe that the inventors, innovators, and builders of our nation were indeed only white.

Early Eurocentric suggestions of racial differences was based on the ideas of Linnacus, who assigned the skin colors, white, red, yellow, and black respectively to Europeans, Native Americans, Asians, and Africans, and attributed several character traits to each race. He thought Europeans were sanguine, brawny, gentle, and inventive; Native Americans were choleric, obstinate, content, and free; Asians were melancholy, rigid, haughty, and covetous; and Africans were phlegmatic, crafty, indolent, and negligent.

`        In American society, the upper class and people of power are unquestionably valued, with little criticism of elitist lifestyles and behaviors, even when their actions or ideas result in inhuman and criminal practices (i.e., colonization, slavery, industrialization, and urbanization, which brought "progress" and wealth to few while creating permanent underclasses. Minority lifestyles are generally stereotyped negatively, that colored people are lazy; but one reason advanced to explain the high unemployment rate among black men is not laziness, but  white people's greater fear of black men.  In negative stereotypes such as being unintelligent, lazy, violent, poor, and unpatriotic, blacks, Hispanics, and Asians are usually more unfavorably stereotyped than whites, or their own group.  Negative stereotypes are most prevalent for blacks and Hispanics and somewhat less strong for Asians, but those of whites are usually favorable.

Another negative stereotype ascribed to black men is typically found in media reporting that represents "lower-class black men" as displaying murderous aggression and self-destructive violence as the modern version of a presumed brutal behavior-complex going back to slavery. The interracial scope of many racial stereotypes such black hypersexuality is a theme that is projected in the U.S., Latin America, and Asia. As society and African-Americans internalize negative racial images, stereotypes are reinforced, and a new cycle of racism is perpetuated.

As America becomes more ethnically and racially diversified, identities are often defined situationally, and in some aspects of new immigrants' everyday lives, race and ethnicity may evolve from ideas learned from workplaces, neighborhoods, and schools. Evidence indicates that developing racial awareness, no matter how subtle and uneven, is an undeniable part of new immigrant's experience. When new identities evolve, including dual or multiple identities, the wider context of racial politics defines the meanings of ethnicity and patriotism.

Cultural and politically influenced images of poverty, welfare, the war on crime and drugs, educational disparities, economic trends, government policies, and even tropical tourist paradises are shaped and popularized by electronic and print media. As a result, many new immigrants to America have already encoded an ideal that accepts the hegemonic views of the United States, which supports "white supremacy", and often blames those classed as black and indigenous for the worsening state of the nation. The process of associating whitening with advancement and darkening with backwardness and stagnation has been facilitated by U.S. military occupation, colonial rule, and/or corporate presence.

Racism is comprised of components; a belief in the innate quality of interracial traits, and a belief in the superiority of one's own race. Negative evaluations of ethnic groups attributes social deviancy rather than cultural or economic status variances. Viewing racial attitudes as results from a zero--sum view of politics; there is the tendency think in terms of "us" and "them", and to see the possibility that their own group could lose something valued to a rival group. Consequently, intergroup conflict and misunderstandings reinforce the persistence of racial stereotypes. Asian and Latin populations in the U.S. has increased the impact of these minorities, and identifying the social construction of these groups and how they coincide with and differ from that of blacks provides a more complete understanding of racial attitudes. By 1992, many African-Americans had reached the top, as many blacks achieved credentials at top universities, corporations, government, and professions which provided them enormous fame, especially from movies, sports, and music . In 1970, 21% of the parents of 13-year-old blacks had post secondary education, but by 1990, 49% had some college education. Among whites, the change over these 20 years was from 41% to 53% . Yet, even with substantial African-American educational advancement, the stereotype of black under achievement still persist, not as the outcome of socio-economics, but as a racial attribute, despite indisputable evidence that students coming from backgrounds of poverty and lack of advantage perform less well on the SAT and are less likely to earn degrees.

Racial preference can be seen in school policies and practices such as tracking, pullouts, and advanced placement courses and programs that foster and promote learning environments favoring those at the higher end of the achievement (and socioeconomic) continuum who have greater access to advanced technological, critical thinking, and conceptual learning strategies. The most unfair and impacting practice is that of tracking, the grouping of students by presumed ability levels. Learning in children is so flexible and responsive to the environment that expectations often become prophecy. Students treated as losers, act like losers; students treated as gifted and talented, act like gifted and talented students.

## Conclusions

Due to the relatively small sample population for this concept paper, only potential trends are identified, and the data analysis did not indicate high degrees of statistical significance. Nonetheless, this paper purports to demonstrate the hypothesis that people of varied skin tones and cultural identification, can and do possess personal racial stereotypes of their own and other groups, and consequently, racial stereotyping is not a practice that can only be ascribed to white people. The process of adopting popular racial stereotypes of the dominant culture in America among minority groups indicate the pernicious and pervasive power of the mass media, educational institutions, and other social forces that reinforce the preponderance of positive stereotypes associated with whites, and negative ones assigned to people of color. The internalization of negative stereotypes of minority groups, by people of color has resulted in the reinforcement of the cycle of racism that persist in America because it accepts white superiority as the national social construction paradigm.

Fairer, truer new images of African-American and minority communities might reduce the probability for urban youth to assume lives of drugs or crime as among their few realistic future options, while increasing the chance that negative stereotypical perceptions of society's    media consumers will challenged and changed. Some African-Americans are doing very well, and they have a strong growing presence at the middle to upper end of the socioeconomic scale, as almost 15% of all African American families have incomes in excess of $50,000. But, as among many groups, black economic achievement is becoming stratified, with wealthier educated members being counterbalanced by larger groups at the lower socioeconomic rungs.

Swartz opines that, "A multicultural education has the potential to rethink and reconstruct Eurocentric curriculum, pedagogy and practices that have historically served to generate supremacist attitudes, feelings, and behaviors". Multicultural education provides information about various cultures, their histories, customs, languages, and traditions, providing learning in an environment where others' values, beliefs, and religions can be accepted and respected. They will need to appreciate differences and be able to be comfortable with individuals who do not look like themselves. It is essential for groups to have the chance for interracial exposure and interaction, to enable them to dispel the prejudices and stereotypes of a racist society and world.

### Appendix I: Survey Data
Tabulation of Responses: Raw Data: N = 110

1.      What do you believe is your inherited genetic "racial" type?
[ 14 ]  African-American    [ 14 ] Asian-American
[ 44 ]  Hispanic  [ 3 ]  Native American
[ 31 ]  Not Listed or Other    [ 4 ] White

2.  What do you think most people and public agencies
    would consider your "race"?
    [ 14 ] African-American   [ 14 ] Asian-American
    [ 61 ] Hispanic  [ 3 ] Native American
    [ 13 ] Not Listed or Other [ 5 ] White

3.  What generation do you represent in your family's
    residence in the U.S.A.?
    [ 45 ] 1st./immigrants  [ 38 ] 2nd/born here
    [ 6 ] 3rd generation  [ 18 ] 4th. gen. or greater

4.  Do you believe that "racism" exist today in America?
    [ 1 ] No       [ 108 ] Yes

5.  Have people outside of your family and friends ever
    treated you differently on account
    of the "race" they perceived you to be?
    [ 91 ] Yes    [ 16 ] No

6.  In your opinion, which "race" is most likely to obtain a
    four year degree in college?
    [ 1 ] African-American  [ 27 ] Asian-American
    [ 0 ] Hispanic  [ 0 ] Native American
    [ 18 ] None, all equal     [ 2 ] Not Listed or Other
    [ 60 ] White

7.  In your opinion, which "race" is most likely to complete
    a graduate school degree?
    [ 0 ] African-American  [ 26 ] Asian-American
    [ 0 ] Hispanic  [ 0 ] Native American
    [ 16 ] None, all equal     [ 3 ] Not Listed or Other
    [ 62 ] White

8. Which "race" is most likely to "get ahead" at work, to be promoted to senior positions?

[ 1 ] African-American  [ 3 ] Asian-American

[ 1 ] Hispanic  [ 2 ] Native American

[ 7 ] None, all equal    [ 3 ] Not Listed or Other

[ 89 ] White

9. Which "race" do you feel gets "most of the best breaks in life"?

[ 4 ] African-American  [ 4 ] Asian-American

[ 0 ] Hispanic  [ 1 ] Native American

[ 11 ] None, all equal    [ 3 ] Not Listed or Other

[ 87 ] White

10. Which "race" do you believe is most likely to become "unemployed"?

[ 55 ] African-American  [ 0 ] Asian-American

[ 23 ] Hispanic  [ 15 ] Native American

[ 14 ] None, all equal    [ 1 ] Not Listed or Other

[ 2 ] White

11. Which "race" do you believe is the most "intelligent"?

[ 2 ] African-American  [ 25 ] Asian-American

[ 3 ] Hispanic  [ 0 ] Native American

[ 73 ] None, all equal    [ 2 ] Not Listed or Other

[ 5 ] White

12. Which "race" do you believe is the most "musically talented"?

[ 27 ] African-American    [ 5 ] Asian-American

[ 13 ] Hispanic   [ 2 ] Native American

[ 55 ] None, all equal      [ 2 ] Not Listed or Other

[ 4 ] White

13. Which "race" do you believe is the most "physically talented"?

[ 53 ] African-American   [ 1 ] Asian-American

[ 3 ] Hispanic   [ 1 ] Native American

[ 44 ] None, all equal      [ 1 ] Not Listed or Other

[ 5 ] White

14. Which "race" do you believe is the most "inventive" or "innovative"?

[ 6 ] African-American   [ 18 ] Asian-American

[ 6 ] Hispanic   [ 4 ] Native American

[ 57 ] None, all equal      [ 3 ] Not Listed or Other

[ 12 ] White

15. Which "race" do you believe is the most "humanitarian"?

[ 6 ] African-American   [ 2 ] Asian-American

[ 17 ] Hispanic   [ 14 ] Native American

[ 55 ] None, all equal      [ 2 ] Not Listed or Other

[ 12 ] White

16. Which "race" do you believe is the most "violent"?

[ 16 ] African-American   [ 1 ] Asian-American

[ 9 ] Hispanic   [ 0 ] Native American

[ 59 ] None, all equal      [ 1 ] Not Listed or Other

[ 13 ] White

17.  Which "race" do you believe is the most "peaceful"?

[ 2 ] African-American  [ 17 ] Asian-American

[ 2 ] Hispanic  [ 24 ] Native American

[ 52 ] None, all equal    [ 4 ] Not Listed or Other

[ 7 ] White

18.  Which "race" do you believe is physically the "best looking"?

[ 10 ] African-American  [ 2 ] Asian-American

[ 27 ] Hispanic  [ 1 ] Native American

[ 50 ] None, all equal    [ 5 ] Not Listed or Other

[ 15 ] White

19.  Which "race" do you believe is the most "rude" and "inconsiderate"?

[ 25] African-American   [ 10 ] Asian-American

[ 4 ] Hispanic  [ 1 ] Native American

[ 53 ] None, all equal    [ 3 ] Not Listed or Other

[ 11 ] White

20.  Which "race" do you believe is the "loudest" and "wildest"?

[ 47 ] African-American  [ 1 ] Asian-American

[ 4 ] Hispanic  [ 0 ] Native American

[ 46 ] None, all equal    [ 3 ] Not Listed or Other

[ 7 ] White

21.  Which "race" do you believe is most likely to become alcoholics?

[ 3 ] African-American  [ 1 ] Asian-American

[ 22 ] Hispanic  [ 17 ] Native American

[ 48 ] None, all equal    [ 6 ] Not Listed or Other
[ 8 ] White

22.   Which "race" do you believe is most likely to become illegal drug users or drug addicts?
[ 26 ] African-American   [ 2 ] Asian-American
[ 12 ] Hispanic   [ 2 ] Native American
[ 53 ] None, all equal    [ 3 ] Not Listed or Other
[ 9 ] White

23.   Which "race" do you believe is most likely to be criminals or be imprisoned?   [ 45 ] African-American
[ 0 ] Asian-American   [ 13 ] Hispanic
[ 1 ] Native American [ 43 ] None, all equal
[ 2 ] Not Listed or Other    [ 6 ] White

24.   Which "race" do you believe is the most likely to be homosexual or bi-sexually preferences?
[ 0 ] African-American   [ 1 ] Asian-American
[ 1 ] Hispanic   [ 0 ] Native American
[ 55 ] None, all equal    [ 2 ] Not Listed or Other
[ 41 ] White

25.   Which "race" do you believe is the most likely to be prejudiced against other races?
[ 8 ] African-American    [ 3 ] Asian-American
[ 2 ] Hispanic   [ 1 ] Native American
[ 43 ] None, all equal    [ 2 ] Not Listed or Other
[ 50 ] White

26. Please check ONE statement that BEST describes your personal beliefs about the concept of "race"?

[ 23 ] Race is skin color and other physical features that are biologically inherited.

[ 9 ] Race includes skin color, and other mental or psychological traits.

[ 23 ] Race is the continent, country, or culture where a person belongs.

[ 42 ] There is no such thing as "race"; all human beings are of the homo-sapiens species.

[ 11 ] I'm not sure whether there's such a thing as "race", or not.

27. If a person of another "race" got a job on account of his "race preference", would you object if he was different from the "race" that identifies you?

[ 42 ] No  [ 59 ] Yes

28. If you had the power to eliminate "race" as a "barrier", would you? [ 21 ] No [ 83 ] Yes

29. Please identify your biological or genetic SEX. [60] Female [48] Male [0] Both [1] None

30. What is your age group?  [ 64 ] 18-25  [ 39 ] 26-39 [ 5 ] 40-61  [ 0 ] 62 or over

## Appendix II: Tabulation of Class Sample Respondents: N=55

1.  What do you believe is your inherited genetic "racial" type?

    [ 9 ] African-American   [ 5 ] Asian-American

    [ 24 ] Hispanic   [ 2 ] Native American

    [ 13 ] Not Listed or Other    [ 2 ] White

2.  What do you think most people and public agencies would consider your "race"?   [ 10 ] African-American

    [ 4 ] Asian-American   [ 34 ] Hispanic

    [ 0 ] Native American   [ 5 ] Not Listed or Other

    [ 3 ] White

3.  What generation do you represent in your family's residence in the U.S.A.?

    [21] 1st./immigrants   [20] 2nd/born here

    [2] 3rd generation   [13] 4th. gen. or greater

4.  Do you believe that "racism" exist today in America?

    [ 0 ] No   [ 55 ] Yes *

5.  Have people outside of your family and friends ever treated you differently on account of the "race" they perceived you to be?       [ 46 ] Yes *   [ 7 ] No

6.  In your opinion, which "race" is most likely to obtain a four year degree in college?

    [ 0 ] African-American   [ 13 ] Asian-American   [ 0 ] Hispanic   [ 0 ] Native American   [ 10 ] None, all equal

    [ 0 ] Not Listed or Other    [ 31 ] White *

7. In your opinion, which "race" is most likely to complete a graduate school degree?

[ 0 ] African-American  [ 8 ] Asian-American  [ 0 ] Hispanic  [ 0 ] Native American  [ 9 ] None, all equal  [ 1 ] Not Listed or Other    [ 35 ] White *

8. Which "race" is most likely to "get ahead" at work, to be promoted to senior positions?

[ 1 ] African-American  [ 0 ] Asian-American  [ 1 ] Hispanic  [ 0 ] Native American  [ 5 ] None, all equal  [ 1 ] Not Listed or Other    [ 46 ] White *

9. Which "race" do you feel gets "most of the best breaks in life"?

[ 2 ] African-American  [ 3 ] Asian-American
[ 0 ] Hispanic  [ 0 ] Native American
[ 3 ] None, all equal    [ 2 ] Not Listed or Other
[ 45 ] White *

10. Which "race" do you believe is most likely to become "unemployed"?

[ 30 ] African-American *  [ 0 ] Asian-American
[ 11 ] Hispanic  [ 7 ] Native American
[ 7 ] None, all equal  [ 1 ] Not Listed or Other
[ 1 ] White

11. Which "race" do you believe is the most "intelligent"?

[ 2 ] African-American    [ 7 ] Asian-American
[ 3 ] Hispanic  [ 0 ] Native American
[ 40 ] None, all equal  *  [ 1 ] Not Listed or Other
[ 2 ] White

12. Which "race" do you believe is the most "musically talented"?

[ 16 ] African-American ** [ 1 ] Asian-American

[ 5 ] Hispanic [ 1 ] Native American

[ 32 ] None, all equal [ 0 ] Not Listed or Other

[ 0 ] White

13. Which "race" do you believe is the most "physically talented"?

[ 30 ] African-American * [ 0 ] Asian-American

[ 1 ] Hispanic [ 0 ] Native American

[ 24 ] None, all equal [ 0 ] Not Listed or Other

[ 0 ] White

14. Which "race" do you believe is the most "inventive" or "innovative"?

[ 6 ] African-American [ 8 ] Asian-American

[ 3 ] Hispanic [ 1 ] Native American

[ 32 ] None, all equal * [ 2 ] Not Listed or Other

[ 3 ] White

15. Which "race" do you believe is the most "humanitarian"?

[ 4 ] African-American ** [ 0 ] Asian-American

[ 10 ] Hispanic [ 6 ] Native American

[ 28 ] None, all equal [ 2 ] Not Listed or Other

[ 5 ] White

16. Which "race" do you believe is the most "violent"?

[ 10 ] African-American [ 0 ] Asian-American

[ 5 ] Hispanic [ 0 ] Native American

[ 34 ] None, all equal     [ 0 ] Not Listed or Other

[ 6 ] White **

17.  Which "race" do you believe is the most "peaceful"?

[ 2 ] African-American  [ 9 ] Asian-American

[ 0 ] Hispanic  [ 9 ] Native American **

[ 31 ] None, all equal     [ 3 ] Not Listed or Other

[ 0 ] White

18.  Which "race" do you believe is physically the "best looking"?

[ 8 ] African-American   [ 0 ] Asian-American

[ 15 ] Hispanic  [ 1 ] Native American

[ 22 ] None, all equal  *  [ 3 ] Not Listed or Other

[ 5 ] White

19.  Which "race" do you believe is the most "rude" and "inconsiderate"?

[ 8 ] African-American    [ 8 ] Asian-American

[ 3 ] Hispanic  [ 0 ] Native American

[ 28 ] None, all equal  *  [ 1 ] Not Listed or Other

[ 6 ] White

20.  Which "race" do you believe is the "loudest" and "wildest"?

[ 27 ] African-American *  [ 0 ] Asian-American

[ 1 ] Hispanic  [ 0 ] Native American

[ 25 ] None, all equal     [ 0 ] Not Listed or Other

[ 0 ] White

21.   Which "race" do you believe is most likely to become alcoholics?

[ 1 ] African-American   [ 0 ] Asian-American
[ 9 ] Hispanic   [ 12 ] Native American **
[28 ] None, all equal   [ 1 ] Not Listed or Other
[ 4 ] White

22.   Which "race" do you believe is most likely to become illegal drug users or drug addicts?

[ 12 ] African-American **  [ 1 ] Asian-American
[ 7 ] Hispanic   [ 2 ] Native American
[ 26 ] None, all equal   [ 0 ] Not Listed or Other
[ 5 ] White

23.   Which "race" do you believe is most likely to be criminals or be imprisoned?

[ 23 ] African-American *  [ 0 ] Asian-American
[ 6 ] Hispanic   [ 1 ] Native American
[ 23 ] None, all equal   [ 1 ] Not Listed or Other
[ 2 ] White

24.   Which "race" do you believe is the most likely to be homosexual or bi-sexually preferenced?

[ 0 ] African-American   [ 1 ] Asian-American
[ 0 ] Hispanic   [ 0 ] Native American   [ 31 ] None, all equal   [ 0 ] Not Listed or Other   [ 21 ] White *

25. Which "race" do you believe is the most likely to be prejudiced against other races?

[ 3 ] African-American    [ 0 ] Asian-American

[ 0 ] Hispanic   [ 0 ] Native American

[ 19 ] None, all equal    [ 1 ] Not Listed or Other

[ 32 ] White *

26. Please check ONE statement that BEST describes your personal beliefs about the concept of "race"?

[ 7 ] Race is skin color and other physical features that are biologically inherited.

[ 3 ] Race includes skin color, and other mental or psychological traits.

[ 11 ] Race is the continent, country, or culture where a person belongs.

[ 29 ] There is no such thing as "race"; all human beings are of the homo-sapiens species. *

[ 5 ] I'm not sure whether there's such a thing as "race", or not.

27. If a person of another "race" got a job on account of his "race preference", would you object if he was different from the "race" that identifies you?

[ 24 ] No  [ 25 ] Yes *

28. If you had the power to eliminate "race" as a "barrier", would you?  [ 16 ] No  [ 36 ] Yes *

29.   Please identify your biological or genetic SEX.
      [27] Female  [27] Male  [0] Both  [0] None
30.   What is your age group?   [ 29 ]  18-25  [ 22 ]  26-39
      [ 3 ]  40-61  [ 0 ]  62 or over

## Bibliography

A. Reynaldo Contreras and Leonard A. Valverde. "The Impact of Brown on
      the Education of Latinos", Journal of Negro Education, Vol. 63,
      Issue 3 (Summer, 1994), 470-481.

Faye V. Harrison. "The Persistent Power of 'Race' in the Cultural and
      Political Economy of Racism", Annual Review of Anthropology,
      Vol. 24 (1995), 47-74.

Kirk A. Johnson.  "Objective News and Other Myths: The Poisoning of
      Young Black Minds",Journal of Negro Education, Vol. 60, Issue 2
      (Summer 1991), 328-341.

Gerard Kleinpenning and Louk Hagendoorn. "Forms of Racism and the
      Cummulative Dimension of Ethnic Attitudes", Social Psychology
      Quarterly, Vol. 56, Issue 1 (Mar., 1993), 21-36.

Michael W. Link and Robert W. Oldendick. "Social Construction and White
      Attitudes toward Equal Opportunity and Multiculturalism", The
      Journal of Politics, Vol. 58, Issue (Feb., 1996), 149-168.

Orlando Patterson. "Backlash", Transition, Vol. 9, Issue 2, 4-26.

Jim Sidanius and Seymour Feshbach, et. al. "The Interface Between
Ethnic and National Attachment: Ethnic Pluralism or Ethnic
Dominance?", Public Opinion Quarterly, Vol. 61, Issue 1, (Spring,
1997), 102-133.

Donald M. Stewart. "Education, Race, and Class: A New Calculus for the
21st Century", Journal of Negro Education, Vol. 52, Issue 2
(Spring, 1993), 113-124.

Ellen Swartz. "Multicultural Education: Disrupting Patterns of Supremacy in
School Curricula, Practices and Pedagogy", Journal of Negro
Education, Vol. 62, Issue 4 (Autumn 1993), 493-506.

Alden T. Vaughn. "From White man to Redskin: Changing Anglo-American
Perceptions of the American Indian", The American Historical
Review, Vol. 87, Issue 4 (Oct., 1982), 917-953.

Thomas C. Wilson. "Cohorts and Prejudice: Whites's Attitudes Toward
Blacks, Hispanics, Jews, and Asians", Public Opinion Quarterly,
Vol. 60, Issue 2 (Summer, 1996), 253-274.

# Chapter Eight - Issues of our Time

As time marches forward, human societies advance technologically; however, the propensity for conflict traps people into complex webs of deception and confusion. Just why don't humans seem able to get along? How much is due to genetic predispositions and survival instincts, versus socially learned conditioned values? What contributes to the formation of attitudes that constitute beliefs relating to?

1.  Fear of the unknown or unfamiliar
2.  Territoriality, property and land ownership
3.  Differentiation, alienation, and segregation
4.  Hierarchical dominance relationships
5.  Protectiveness of loves ones & own group
6.  Affiliation with other familiar humans
7.  Jealousy, anger, envy and negative emotions
8.  Self-centeredness and selfishness
9.  Intolerance and rejection of differences
10. Aggression, predatory and violent behavior
11. Superiority versus inferiority
12. Cultural, racial, and ethnic pride
13. Class, race, sex, age, disability, ethnic, and intellectual discrimination
14. Religious pursuits, beliefs, and superstition
15. Group, peer, and media pressure to conform to norms
16. Needing predictability in dealing with a matrix of needs

17. Believing in authority figures, governments, schools, and the media
18. Greed, hoarding, and competitiveness
19. Desire for power and control over others
20. Wastefulness, destructiveness, excesses, and compulsiveness

The interaction and prevalence of human attitudes has resulted in the development of complex and apparently unsolvable problems. When human societies begin to focus on finding realistic answers to many of the following problems, there may be hope yet, that the human species may survive another century.

1. What types of jobs will be eliminated by technology, outsourcing, and decreased demand for various products and services?
2. What new jobs will be created as a result of technology, terrorism, and new consumer needs?
3. What are the negative consequences of globalization versus the positive results? How will globalization contribute to the rise of oligarchies, increased prices, manipulated supply shortages, decreased choices, and permanently lost occupations and jobs?
4. What are potentially positive affects of globalization? Will it bring more efficiency, more coordinated and equitable distribution of resources and products, and minimizing wastage?

5. Is nuclear proliferation, conflict, and global thermonuclear war likely?

6. How relevant is education as we know it? How can we improve it and prepare students for an unpredictable future? What is the purpose, goals, and transition that education must endure to remain relevant as computers and high tech makes human knowledge broad and instantaneous?

7. What areas of environmental protection are "essential" for the ecosystem, human survival, and quality of life?

8. How do we control geometric world population growth?

9. What is the appropriate balance between personal privacy and the state's need to know to provide adequate homeland security and protections

10. What can be done to shrink government and the voluminous accrual of laws on the books?

11. What is mankind's collective vision of the future of human beings?

12. How can world governments act in cooperation to "lift the tide" to reduce great economic disparities between the rich and poor, to eliminate unequal distribution of resources and wealth, and to eliminate poverty and disease?

13. What new "survival paradigm" versus the "hard work & zero-sum game" paradigm would more appropriately address future trends and changes?

14. How can we improve social interactions, relationships, and civility?

15. How can the justice system become more "just" and efficient?

16. How do we adequately provide for the elderly, infirmed, and disabled?

17. How do we provide adequate low and reasonably priced housing?

18. How can we eliminate terrorism before it eliminates civilization?

19. How do we encourage teens to develop more responsible attitudes for their own lives and that of others?

20. What are the solutions to the abortion, right to life, assisted suicide issues?

21. How can government bureaucracy become more efficient and effective?

22. How can corruption be weeded out from government and corporations?

23. How can the cycle of gangs, poverty, and violence be broken?

24. How can legislators make more sensible and appropriate laws that serve the public interest instead of special interest?

25. How can people become more content, self-accepting, and happy?

26. What events are likely to cause TEOTWAWKIT by the year 2020?
27. How can we improve human contact and relationships?
28. What is fantasy versus reality nowadays?
29. What would happen if everyone decided to be completely honest?
30. What benefits can we obtain from space exploration and travel?

Topics that come up on a daily basis attack our senses and sensibilities. Here's an abbreviated list of just a few of the concerns that we are inundated by in our minds.

| | | | |
|---|---|---|---|
| 1. | Education | 2. | Crime |
| 3. | Warfare | | |
| 4. | Pollution | 5. | Pornography |
| 6. | Drugs | | |
| 7. | Immigration | 8. | Quality of life |
| 9. | Health | | |
| 10. | Excessive greed | 11. | Unemployment |
| 12. | Racism | | |
| 13. | Sexual slavery | 14. | Sexism |
| 15. | Exploitation | | |
| 16. | Sexual harassment | 17. | Deception |
| 18. | Stupidity | | |
| 19. | Lying | 20. | Dishonesty |
| 21. | Civility | | |

22. White power     23. Anti-Semitism
24. Zionism
25. Iraq ambushes     26. Special interests
27. Politics
28. Consumption     29. Employment
30. Career
31. Ethnic pride     32. Citizenship
33. Patriotism
34. Intolerance     35. Overpopulation
36. Disabilities
37. Abortion     38. Suicide
39. Immorality
40. Reproductive rights 41. Sexual preference
42. Alcohol
43. Smoking     44. Social norms
45. Media bias
46. Homeland security 47. Poverty
48. Diseases
49. Privacy rights     50. Violence
51. Technology
52. Space exploration 53. Destructiveness
54. Energy costs
55. Age of consent     56. Alternative energy
57. Death
58. Incarceration     59. Credit problems
60. Work ethic

61. Rude & toxic folks
62. Mandatory jail
63. 3 strikes law
64. Escapism
65. Recreation
66. Rest
67. Relationships
68. Loneliness
69. Alienation
70. Sexuality
71. Spirituality
72. Religion
73. Freedom of choice
74. Freeway traffic
75. Justice
76. Fairness
77. Court system
78. UFO's/ET's
79. Zero-sum game
80. Police brutality
81. Cop chases
82. Gang violence
83. Bureaucracy
84. Boredom
85. Winning
86. Losing
87. Cheating
88. Money
89. Gambling
90. Lottery
91. Sex
92. Emotional needs
93. Child abuse
94. Creation vs evolution
95. Elderly abuse
96. Threats
97. Spousal abuse
98. Science and reality
99. Rage

| | |
|---|---|
| 100. Uncertainty | 101. Aggressive driving |
| 102. Infinity | |
| 103. Blood pressure | 104. Dieting |
| 105. Appearance | |
| 106. Stem cell research | 107. Genetic modifications |
| 108. Toxic foods | |
| 109. Cloning | 110. New world order |
| 111. Globalization | |
| 112. Unemployment | 113. Parking spaces |
| 114. End times | |
| 115. Teen rebellion | 116. IMF |
| 117. WTO | |
| 118. WMDs | 119. TEOTWAWKI |
| 120. Terrorism | |
| 121. Mind control | 122. Witchcraft |
| 123. Prophesy | |
| 124. Religious conflict | 125. Television shows |
| 126. Emails | |
| 127. Banking | 128. Postal mail |
| 129. Family | |
| 130. Shopping | 131. Grocery stores str |
| 33. rush hour commute | |
| 134. Wardrobe | 135. Bills and payments |
| 136. Work & career | |
| 137. Auto repairs | 138. Crazy people |
| 139. Fees & fines | |

140.  Government taxes   141.  Parking tickets

142.  Entertainment

143.  Balance checkbook 144.  Overdrawn fees

145.  Tiredness

146.  Being in a rush    147.  Stressed out

148.  Anxiety

149.  Frustration        150.  Depression

151.  Anger

152.  Eating choices     153.  Social contact

154.  Avoidance

155.  Political correctness156.  Comparing oneself

157.  Enjoyment

158.  Current events     159.  Investments

160.  Death

During the past decade, 10% of these topics did not exist.  It seems that every year, there's more topics that clutter our minds, hearts, and lives.  One hundred years ago, there were 100 less topics of concern, because they didn't exist. Anything over 10 topics of concern per day has the potential of creating extra stress, distraction, and defocuses our lives from the more important issues.  During simpler times, people probably only had to deal with half a dozen issues each day, such as tending the crops and animals, going in to eat when called, fetching water for bathing, resting and sleep, and family.  Is that six?  They were probably happier during those simpler days, and less preoccupied about so many extraneous issues that plague us today. I can't wait for scientist to discover how to send us back in time to simpler days.

## Chapter Nine - Destroying American Society

Bin Laden, Al Qaida, and global terrorism is only one strategic plan to attempt to weaken The United States of America, our federal government, American culture, our freedoms, liberties, and way of life. The long-range goals of various anti-American conspirators are simple, as we are witnessing the results of its insidious plot, as our society continues to decay in all areas.

1.　Social decay through propagating disunity among Americans.
　　a.　Fuel racism by blaming whites for all of society's ills, thus driving a wedge between minority races and the majority.
　　b.　Promote immorality and divisive cultural-ethnic-racial-sex conflicts by legalizing homosexual marriages, pornography, illegal immigration, affirmative action, late term abortion, and encouraging degeneration through mass media, television programs, music, and popular culture.

c.    Promote interracial conflict by creating
      ineffective minority hand out programs that pits
      one race against another.

d.    Create disrespect for authority and government
      by gradually outlawing basic freedoms, and
      creating too much red tape.

e.    Cause ethical and moral decay by outlawing
      reasonable corporal punishment of children for
      destructive conduct, when reasonable
      punishment by parents and teachers could keep
      certain students from lives of crime.  Instead,
      disrespectful children later become
      rebellious teens who eventually spend much of
      their adult lives in prison, becoming subjected to
      highly violent environments that far exceeds the
      penalty of a loving spanking when it could
      have made a positive difference in their young
      lives.

f.    Suppress and ridicule good citizenship and
      patriotism, while promoting sex, violence, and
      greed as a "cool" and desirable lifestyle.

g.    Resist progressive changes to the education
      system, such as school vouchers.  Mix all
      children into template classes, where
      disinterested and disruptive children ruin the
      environment for students who wish to learn.
      Penalize the teachers by making them

suspect for every frivolous and false accusation from dysfunctional students.

2.   Political decay by the media and universities encouraging distrust of government, particularly the federal government.

    a.   Special interest groups and political lobbyists entice and corrupt government officials, politicians, and bureaucrats.

    b.   Alienate citizens from governance by making them feel disinterested and hopeless to positively change policies. When citizens no longer monitor government activities, there is greater latitude for corruptive influences to make significant inroads.

    c.   Persuade corrupted legislators and agency chiefs to make policies that favor special interest groups, while punishing citizens, thereby transferring citizens' money to special interest groups, corrupt corporate executives and economic elites.

3.   Economic decay is evidenced by a strategy of wealth transfer from the working middle class to special interests elites.

a.    The U.S. A. is treated as just another consumer market for exploitation and wealth building by the elites, thus the ends justify the means, and patriotism is not a concern.

b.    Swindle retirees of their life savings and pensions through clever investment ruses and fraud.  Enron, Arthur Andersen and Merrill Lynch corruption is only the tip of the iceberg. Law enforcement must identify, by using reverse phone trees and wire tapes, to obtain evidence to justify the round up of top executives from this conspiratorial network to prevent them from corrupting every person and corporation that they touch and bribe; otherwise, they and those like them will breed like cockroaches, and soon it will be near impossible to isolate and catch them.

c.    Use technology to replace American workers, to maximize corporate profits and compensation to greedy CEOs, CFOs, Board Chairs and Directors under the guise of necessity and competitive survivability, instead of admitting wanton greed.

d.    Outsource manufacturing and white-collar high tech jobs to cheap labor markets, even if the consequence is harmful to the U.S. economy.

e.    Concentrate control of strategic industries, raw materials, and consumer markets to MNCs whose executives have no loyalty to America, but only to personal wealth building.

f.    Destabilize the U.S. dollar, cause sudden massive monetary devaluations, and de-dollarize international trade when the monetary and trade imbalances makes currencies ripe for hedge

4.    International relations decay by attempting to discredit, isolate and alienate President Bush, the CIA and our government on the world stage and among our supposed allies.

a.    Implement anti-Bush, anti-CIA, and anti-American propaganda tactics.

b.    Use domestic and international news media to foment anti-American and anti-CIA sentiments through biased news editing, reporting, and commentary that is represented as factual news.

c.    Foment international violence, conflicts and insurgency to test American diplomatic and military response, and to stretch out all of America's military resources abroad, thereby weakening the U.S. frontlines and logistics.

d.    Criticize U.S. response as being either too little too late, too heavy-handed and unilateralist, or too insensitive, or whatever slant is necessary to discredit America's good intentions and good deeds abroad.

e.    Foster anti-American sentiments to unify different political and religious camps by recognizing the U.S.A. as their common foe, by applying the "Your enemy's enemy is your friend" principle. This strategy is being used among Islamic states, anti-Semitic groups, and terrorist networks. A unified Europe, Sino-Russian rapprochement, and a unified South America all present future potential hot spots in fomenting future anti-American sentiments around the world.

5.    Military decay through compromise, overpriced military contracts, spying, contracting out to foreign companies, conflicts of interest among current and retired brass and civilian administrators, and wasting precious military funds on various kickback schemes, while American troops fail to receive the required equipment to protect their lives and to make them successful in their military missions.

a.    U.S. dependency on foreign manufacturers, suppliers, and raw materials needed for military hardware and systems.

b. Spies and moles planted in sensitive government agencies and committees with oversight over intelligence, military technology, procurement, and operations.

c. Government contracts and subcontracts that allow foreign corporations (thus governments) to monitor our military and government communication through service providers of email, phone, fax, hardware and software.

d. Installation of "back door" and "trap door" computer chips or spy software in military and government computer networks and equipment, such as computers, planes, trucks, offices, and ships for spying.

e. Integration of "override" chips or software programs into military weapons and communications systems to permit partial or complete take over, sabotage, or destruction of vulnerable military systems, such as virtual battlefield and the Joint Attack Fighter.

f. Install spy technology into sensitive American facilities, vehicles, buildings, and offices through construction, artwork, furniture, equipment, housekeeping and security contractors and suppliers.

People who doubt that these secretive agendas are in operation need only open their eyes to the decay that has inched its way into American society, laws, corporations, and culture since the end of the Vietnam War. We can not solve our nation's problems, protect our homeland and way of life, and restore civility, morality and ethics to our society until we recognize, rather than deny that a serious and grave set of problems exist that is being fostered by our enemies, both here at home and abroad. Then we must be willing to pay the cost of placing the best people and resources that would be required to attack the problem with effective solutions.

# Chapter Ten – Empowerment

Ownership rights, territoriality, socialization, and boredom have been the underlying causes of conflict and disparity to afflict human beings in modern times. Ownership, particularly land ownership has created a system of inequity, injustice, and oppression that has been the obstacle to the realization of peace and cooperation. These roots have created the environment for continued conflict, as human beings have become defined according to their relationship to land and property ownership. The ridiculousness of the concept of land ownership lies in the fact that the land was already here for billions of years before humans walked the earth, and will be here billions of years after human extinction. Consequently, the notion of land ownership is an illusion, and serves only to support a status quo structure that creates an elitist system that separates value between those who make claim to an illusion of ownership, versus those who make no such claims. Consequently, nations, peoples, and ethnic groups constantly fight over territory and what they claim is ownership rights to land, an illusion.

The basic concept of ownership of any type is very infantile and perverse. Let's take for instance a child when it is playing with a toy. If another person takes away the toy from the child before it is ready to release or before it loses interest in the object, it will protest, and soon it learns to say,

"It's mine!" and begin to claim ownership to that object. This fear of loss has created what is prevalent in societies, as the perception of a "zero-sum game", that someone else's gain becomes one's personal loss. This entire state of mind and mind-set contributes to the development of greed and unregulated selfishness, coveting, and jealousy in the human psyche, which in turn results in conflict, violence, and war.

But what would happen to people and the world, were infants allowed to explore and to discover and become satiated, and not to experience withdrawal and rejection or fear of punishment? What if children were raised to experience and expect abundance instead of limited resources? Truly, we live in a world of abundant resources; one only needs to take a jet plane ride, or step on board an ocean liner to realize that simple fact. What one sees from the air or out at sea is thousands and thousands of apparently endless square miles of natural resources, interspersed here and there by small specks of what we call cities, concentrations of humanity.

Especially with technological advances, both existing, under development, and of the future yet to be realized or discovered, it appears the concept of a "zero-sum game" is somewhat obsolete, and actually, it was never a valid concept to begin with, as abundance is the natural state of our planet and the universe. The only reason why there are shortages is due to the disequilibria caused by inequality, unequal distribution, paranoid hoarding, and greed that is caused by the socialized desire for ownership gone rampant and out of control.

All the political systems of the world have become drunk and corrupt with the concept and practice of ownership. The idea of ownership is so perverse that it actually made all the political systems of "isms" and philosophical concepts become corrupted and ineffective in real world application. The concept of ownership is so perverted that political and philosophical ideas are assigned to individuals, as if they can actually own thoughts, where the rest who adopted ideas became mere brainless followers and renters of concepts. Certainly, as ideas have no real permanence, and change over the passing of time, except that they are rehashed again and again, it is ridiculous to ascribe ownership to such ephemeral and nebulous processes as thinking, thoughts, and ideas.

Looking back on political systems, why didn't communism work? The answer isn't so much that Ronald Reagan and George Bush Sr. caused the collapse of the communist system in the Soviet Union, but rather, economic collapse was precipitated by the lengthy and expensive nuclear arms race against the West, along with rampant internal corruption that caused the Soviet Union to devolve back into ethnic nation-states. Communism, which to the working masses at one time looked promising on paper, where ownership of land and the means of production supposedly belonged to the people, failed because in reality, the common faceless masses never really owned anything. It was the powerful and repressive Politburo and Communist Party members who ran the state, controlled and manipulated production, property, and land ownership to the advantage of their indigenous elites, and not for the benefit of average citizens, but often to the disadvantage of the proletariat who comprised the masses of working class people.

Under the system of socialism, ownership is given to the state as the caretaker and trustee of society, or the social order. In fact, what actually results is the creation of a class of elites who exert control, influence, and manage the resources of ownership. Pure capitalism is a system where ownership is the means to an end, and in its present form is becoming a system gone wild and often out of control, creating such disparate and dichotomous social conditions that can only be described by the cliché, "The rich get richer, and the poor get poorer." The wealthy really don't give a damn about the poor in the current greed-ridden capitalistic system. Many corporate CEO's receive upwards to 1000 times the compensation that is typically paid to rank and file workers, and the ENRON scandal indicates that some corporate executives are not bashful to "cook the books" in collusion with accountancy firms, to make stock market and financial decisions based upon insider trading information, and to contribute generously to the campaign funds of politicians, who are then coaxed to influence regulatory agencies to turn a blind eye to potential and actual cases of conflict of interests and corruption.

Human life, as with all other life, is no more than a temporary occupying of time and space. In order to combat boredom, people create civilizations and games to occupy time and to have things to do in the course of pursuing basic needs, as people create various relationships to fill the hours of their lives. Human beings are always looking for something to do because we have not accepted nature and everything for what it is, and to live naturally and therefore, people have created alternative realities. As long as people continue to build alternative realities that define their environments to reflect their own self interests and their ability or inability to benefit from their immediate environments, then we have a situation where individually and culturally, the perception of reality becomes so deceptive that it creates formidable obstacles to interaction. Consequently, people lose clarity in their relationships, and instead must go through layers of mind-speak and other distorted perceptions, concepts, and thoughts in order to reach a point where people are able to recognize where others begin.

People who are able to recognize social conditioning, and aspects of civilization and socialization for what it really is, don't feel compelled to define themselves by those biased values, but only by the relationship to their activities and not as definition of self-identity. When we recognize and eventually make conscious decisions to strip ourselves of our subconscious conditioning, then we come closer to recognizing who we truly are, what we want from life in terms of occupying time and space, other than applying external influences that color and taint our perceptions of the true reality. Once we've freed ourselves from the social and cultural definitions of our inner identity, we have a real opportunity to recognize our own personality and character traits, desires, idiosyncrasies, and other aspects that make us even more unique than that of every blade of grass in the world.

What do people say when they are asked, "Who are you when you're not being a [whatever occupation]?" It's probably difficult for most people to define who they are without referring to what they do for a job, or their domestic role, or what things they enjoy doing. Most people give little thought to who they are, and what they really want versus copying what society, the media, and others have defined as being of value. But of value to whom? Who's making money behind the creation of needs, defining value, and therefore benefit from the satisfaction of artificially manufactured needs that become economic opportunity?

It is also a truism that the more time that a person spends on a particular activity, focusing, concentrating, and practicing a specific pattern of behavior, that for no other reason than trial and error, a person will become more proficient at that activity. In this way, we look at the operation of greed and ownership in the same respect. Society and people spend so much investment of time and energy in the practice of activities related to ownership and greed that elite groups of people have become very proficient at making money and owning property, while the poor have few skills in that arena. In fact, it would be a sophomoric understatement to claim that the primary pursuit of people in contemporary life revolves around obtaining money one way or another. As we look back on thousands of years of civilizations, we find that ownership of property, land, animals, and people have been a common phenomenon that caused misery.

Which brings us to the issue of, "Why should anyone care?" Ironically, people tend to have their priorities reversed in this illusory reality. People care about what other people think about them, in the clothes they wear, the type of car they drive, and the career position they occupy, particularly in terms of the level of monetary compensation they've achieved. As a result, the vast majority of socialized and culturally conditioned people define themselves, their self-identity, and self-image by what other people are thinking, and by social norms. However, in the case of caring for the substantive issues of the world, of the great harm and suffering that a global system of inequities causes through the system of disparate ownership structures, most people don't seem to give a damn. Rather, they are eager to write off the poor as being lazy and undeserving of a decent humanitarian life, while the wealthy elites are glorified and valued as having attained social stature that justifies their positions of privilege, control, insensitivity, and even gross immoralities.

Were it not for a world system based upon ownership and socially constructed norms, people would possess the liberty to pursue their happiness without artificial constraints that primarily serves to exploit the masses in order to benefit the comparative few. What would be a vision of an alternative reality free of the brainwashed illusions that contemporary humans have come to accept as being real? Perhaps we can consider the following wish list, not because it may appear idealistic or unrealistic, but because it is actually possible and attainable were the human spirit to be aptly applied. Unchanged, our current state of affairs will likely lead to the eventually reality, that of genocide, nuclear, biological or genetic warfare, and annihilation. Is it unreasonable to hope for a better world where the following vision can be real? Why can't we have a world where,

1) People would accept each individual as being wonderfully unique and celebrate difference and diversity as the natural state and heritage of humanity?

2) People would stop comparing themselves to others, and what they own, where there is no practice of concepts such as "status", "norms", "superiority", "inferiority", and "ridicule"?

3) People would have the freedom to pursue their wildest dreams as long as they don't intentionally hurt others, and where capitalism can become a tool of empowerment without oppression and exploitation?

4) People would respect each other's right to self-determination, and not feel offended, jealous, rejected, hurt, or angered when another person chooses not to associate or to be friends?

5) People would be helped to determine their strengths, talents, and weaknesses, and be allowed to improve themselves in their lives and careers?

6) People would be helped to discover careers that have meaning, that permits them to feel passion, have vision, and commit themselves to a purpose far beyond just keeping busy to earn a paycheck?

7) Every person born into this world is guaranteed the basic rights to survival, food, shelter, education, healthcare, freedom, safety, and the pursuit of happiness?

8) People would be honest with themselves and others in a civil and courteous manner, so human interaction can become reflective of reality, and not illusory, deceptive, or manipulative?

9) Divisive categorical labels will become non-existent; that concepts such as gender, race, nationality, age, disability, sexual preference, class, and cultural distinctions no longer become the basis of identity or social value?

10) Conflict, drama, violence, hatred, and war would be replaced by cooperation, passion, kindness, respect, love and peace?

Why can't we nurture the development of self-empowered individuals who,

1) Have an accurate sense of true self-identity that explains one's position and niche in relation to others and society, without having to validate oneself with norms?

2) Have a clear understanding of personal feelings, beliefs, desires, and preferences, and the reasons why?

3) Recognize the structures and values of socially constructed systems that regulate society and interpersonal relations and interactions, and not be a slave to them?

4) Pursue self-expression without hesitation, restraint, or self-censorship, as long as there is no intent to harm others?

5) Have courage to stand up and be counted for one's principles, to be different from the crowd, if necessary to express one's passions and honest beliefs?

6) Are egalitarian, fair-minded, open-minded, and who do not attempt to force one's personal views on others; people who live and let live?

7) Do not accept prejudices, stereotypes, and injustices as the basis to judge or deal with others, and who speaks up to protest the practice of injustice?

8) Are empathetic, compassionate, and forgiving, with healthy humanitarian orientation toward kindness, sharing, and caring?

9) Recognize the motives of others and constructively engages competing interests to obtain cooperation and mutual benefits in a world of abundance?

10) Recognizes human drives, needs, imperfections, weaknesses, propensities, and conditioning, and tries to improve life's environment by accepting reality as it unfolds without expectations of egocentric outcomes, but for community benefit?

11)    Just want to get along with their fellow human
       beings, instead of competing?

So what's so wrong with seeking an alternative
paradigm to the existing state of human affairs?  Unless we
want conflict, violence, and war to continue to rule the world,
we must seek alternative realities before it's too late for the
survival of human beings.  As the state of world affairs
remains conflictual, is the likelihood of a thermal nuclear war
within ten years likely?

# Chapter Eleven - An Ideal World

In an ideal world, which is worth striving for, every person born would have the basic entitlement to adequate:

| | | | |
|---|---|---|---|
| 1. | Food | 2. | Shelter |
| 3. | Education | 4. | Medical care |
| 5. | Love and affection | 6. | Religious freedom |
| 7. | Reasonable liberties | 8. | Non-violence |
| 9. | Protection from exploiters | 10. | Association freedom |
| 11. | Pursuit of personal values | 12. | Full employment |
| 13. | Respect and dignity | 14. | Non-intimidation |

How could societies offer these basic entitlements?

1. Food based on nutritional standards, supplemented by governments
2. Shelter based on govt./private/self-help partnership programs
3. Educational goals that provide choice, emphasize functional knowledge
   and skills development, good citizenship and ethics, and career goals
4. Medical care that is affordable, effective, and protects against catastrophes
5. Love and affection from effective parents, guardians, and community
6. Peaceful religious practices of any type should be allowed; violence not

7. Freedoms of speech, expression, assembly and press if not destructive
8. Protection from violent offenders; incarcerate and reprogram their brains
9. Non-exploitation through honest, transparent, and non-corrupt practices
10. Freedom to choose associates and to disapprove association
11. Pursuit of personal choices and happiness as long as not harming others
12. Sustainable employment at "living wages" and minimal taxation
13. Respect, dignity, and civility; "do unto others as they should do to you."
14. Freedom from fear and intimidation by bullies, criminals, and authorities

The historical paradigm has always been the survival of the most ruthless, predatory, and brutal people. Human evolution has hopefully raised collective consciousness to recognize that force, violence, and intimidation is barbaric and should be avoided. Unfortunately, lip service too often gives way to bad habits.

But what if the world's economic and political leaders and elites would make changes that could benefit humanity, while continuing to add profits to their assets and investment portfolios? What areas are ripe for positive change that is both good economics and good politics?

Human Rights
1.    Basic freedoms of speech, association, and press
2.    Equal vote to elect government officials
3.    Protection from predators; physical and economic.
4.    Basic sustenance; food, water & shelter.
5.    Right to privacy & sex preference.
6.    Private property ownership rights

Eligibility for the above rights (reference above numbers)
1.    Everyone
2.    Age 16 if pass history test, or 18 & up
3.    Everyone
4.    Everyone
5.    Puberty if at least 12 and mentally/emotionally mature
6.    Everyone

Reproductive Rights and Limitations
1.    Genetic testing to correct fetal defects.
2.    Financially capable to raise children.
3.    Emotionally stable & mature (pass tests).
4.    Parenting education & skills (pass tests).

5.      Family-oriented lifestyles.

6.      Marriage & parenthood contracts.

7.      Limitation criteria on number of children.

8.      Penalties for violation, up to sterilization.

Eligibility Benchmarks to above

1.      Income criteria

2.      National quotas

3.      Age limits: >18 <50

4.      Health of parents

5.      Genetic assessment

Employment Rights; options available but not mandatory

1.      Aptitude, interests, & personality assessed

2.      Career guidance and curriculum choices

3.      Career networking & specialized training

4.      Pre-application to employers

5.      Application to employers

6.      Unemployment insurance benefits.

Shelter Programs

1.      Safe neighborhoods

2.      Block associations, watch, and beautification

3.      Community protection and development

4.      Rent control; reasonable and affordable

5.      Housing and environmental standards.

6.      All areas are subject to minimal national standards.

Religious Rights

1. Freedom to worship in private locations
2. Prayer break time at work (non-paid)
3. Religious release time after school
4. Only non-violent religions qualify
5. Religious tolerance.
6. All areas are subject to minimal national standards

Educational Rights

1. Mandatory education age
2. Optional education age
3. College eligibility
4. Trade & technical school eligibility

Healthcare Rights

1. Catastrophic hospitalization
2. Medical maintenance treatment
3. Medicines and technology
4. Affordable, uniform and cap on maximum costs

Ownership Rights

1. Individual, group, association, community, and government
2. Computerized national database
3. Assignment, inheritance, in perpetuity
4. Trusts and foundations
5. 5. Limitation on monopolies & oligarchies.

## Wealth Building Rights & Limits

1. Patent laws revised to credit original ideas
2. Non-exploitation fair trade practices
3. Non-predatory fair business practices
4. Anti-corruption, anti-crime, legal seizures
5. Anti-fraud, honest advertising & practices

## Environmental Rights

1. Clean air, water, soil, neighborhoods, and highways
2. Safe foods, disease free meats & produce
3. GM food safety certified before release
4. Conservation
5. Recycling
6. Restoration and renewal

## Governance Rights

1. Internet voting with secure biometric ID
2. Internet polls on legislative initiative votes
3. Direct democracy Internet voting on issues
4. Simplify & purge laws that are outdated
5. Statute of limits on laws except murder
6. Public education & access to all laws
7. Outlaw special interest lobbying smoozing and financial contributions; audit lobbyists.

Who stands to benefit from these humanitarian, social, economic, political, religious, and environmental rights? In most cases, all sectors would benefit; the wealthy, middle class, the poor and responsible politicians. What are the probable economic impact on jobs and profits? Which sectors of the population and economy stands to gain most? Every sector rich and poor.

American society is often criticized by foreigners, social advocates, and environmentalists as being wasteful, overly materialistic, and destructive. The poor complain they don't have equal opportunities, and the wealthy claim they are overburdened with taxes that are used to support the poor. The working class feels exploited by both the giveaway programs for the poor, and the huge tax loopholes enjoyed by the rich, paid for by their hard earned taxes paid to support government.

Benefits of positive changes to the social, economic and political structure offers opportunities for diverse segments of society, representing individuals, groups, corporations, government, professionals, the wealthy, middle-class and the poor. Too often, beneficiaries of expenditures and tax benefits fear changes would reduce their personal gains; however, in most cases, the status quo is not threatened because new opportunities usually arise. The shifting of focus to provide positive and constructive options and changes to the status quo can act to improve society and therefore provide ample benefits to all sectors. The option is to retain the inefficient, wasteful and ineffective system that exists now.

# Chapter Twelve - Alternative Realities

As technology has caused sweeping changes to the social and cultural fabrics of almost all nations who have embraced the capitalistic path, the peoples of the world have become enticed and mesmerized by existing ideological paradigms that while stimulating the consumerism and wealth building for the elites, have done little to solve persistent global problems.

What if the world as it has become could have started off differently?

| Current Paradigms | Alternative Paradigms |
| --- | --- |
| This is the only program | Is this the best solution? |
| It only works this way | Is there a better way ? |
| Stakeholders benefit most | Everybody benefits |
| Pro sport heroes | Why heroes to look up to? |
| War heroes | Why honor killing? |
| Reality shows | It's fake called reality |
| Organized religions | Less brainwashing dogma |
| Video games | Get off your ass |
| Stock market | Outlaw fraudulent products |
| Commercial television | Public decides programming |
| Banks | Government accounting |
| Bank fees | Based on actual service costs |
| News media sound bytes | Networks need not cover same stories |
| Special interest lobbyists | Eliminate junkets, gifts, and favors |
| Corporations | Same as people with no special rights |
| Monopolies | At least a dozen competitors needed |
| Oligarchies | Must divest more than 50% |
| Unemployment | Better matching by computer software |
| Unemployment statistics | Transparent and accurate true rates |
| Politicians | Litmus test – honesty and integrity |
| Primary elections/caucuses | Replace with secured internet voting |
| Political commercials | Banned between 6am and 10pm |

| Current Paradigms | Alternative Paradigms |
|---|---|
| Bureaucracy | Public feedback monthly reports |
| Underemployment | Better matching of skills to jobs |
| Hard work cultural value | Work smarter and not harder |
| De facto segregation | Freedom of association |
| Non-discrimination | Equal access but no special quotas |
| Classroom education | Web based education with mentors |
| Name brand products | No deceptive packaging or claims |
| Private property | Limits to government intrusions |
| Home Ownership | 1 year no foreclosures if 50% pymts |
| Money | Digital cash via smart phones/cards |
| Credit interest rates | Limits on usurious rates |
| Classes | Not defined as all part of continuum |
| Race | Not defined as all part of humanity |
| Gender | Not defined as it shouldn't matter |
| Sex | Not defined as individual freedom |
| Ethnicity | Not defined as it shouldn't matter |
| Culture | What individuals prefer, not norms |
| Nationalism | Don't go overboard to make enemies |
| Social Conditioning | Individual choice, not social norms |
| Rewards | People should get what they earn |
| Punishments | People should get what they deserve |
| Elitism | Mirror mirror on the wall. Get over it. |
| Poverty | Equates to inhumanity, so fix it |
| Equality | Open opportunities, individual effort |
| Fairness | Transparency in all dealings & hirings |
| Hiring interviews | More object computer scoring of skills |
| High interest loans | Outlaw as usurious |
| Laws | Too many intrusive outdated & stupid |
| Legal system | Less lawyers, more computer software |
| Court system | Unclog from all but serious crimes |
| Prison system | Keep the violent and dangerous ones |
| Homelessness | Community job programs to help |
| Health insurance | Justify rates for services vs. profits |
| Patent laws | Simplify, reduce costs, and encourage |
| Boredom | Free info on web depending on mood |
| Marketing | No deception or false claims – be real |
| Advertising | No privacy intrusions via Internet |
| Product upgrades | New gadgets and tricks worth buying? |
| Planned obsolescence | Must guarantee parts for 10 years |
| Planned deterioration | Must guarantee to last at least 5 years |
| Social standards | Everyone is different & has self-worth |
| Insecurities | Conquer fear of the unknown |
| Fads and trends | Ok that people like to follow the latest |
| Needs fulfillment | Individual preferences respected |
| Exporting economic base | Limit outsourcing of jobs to <10%/yr. |

| Current Paradigms | Alternative Paradigms |
| --- | --- |
| Corporate corruption | CEOs held responsible if not prohibit |
| Government corruption | Department heads held responsible |
| Economic system | Free market capitalism – no cheating |
| Terrorism | Stop meddling in other nations' affairs |
| I.D. technology | ID chip everybody who wants it |
| Cell phone tracking | Defaults to no GPS, must choose it |
| Crime | Less laws, less crime. Go after violent |
| Violence | Put them predators away for long time |
| Refugees | One year maximum temporary status |
| Starvation | We can do much better– very wasteful |
| Globalization | One World Order is dangerous control |
| WMDs | Outlaw and destroy all WMDs globally |
| Space exploration | Stimulates economy, human progress |
| Missile defense shield | Every nation should have it |
| Creating new jobs | No government impediments |
| Mining the earth | 95% of resources still untapped |
| Global governance | National sovereignty & regional control |
| Conflict | Look for compromise not principles |
| Warfare | No more false flag wars for oil |
| GPS | Consumers have rights to reject |
| Alternative energies | Must develop for long term benefits |
| Fossil fuels | New technologies to clean up usage |
| GM foods | Making kids autistic?  Controls needed |
| Genetic engineering | Make a better stronger human being |
| Cloning | Reproducing greatness but only once |
| VR | Too much as people get reality check |
| Drug abuse | Drugs without negative side effects |
| Alcoholism | Remove negative side effects |
| Gambling | Casinos to put cap on max daily bets |
| Prostitution | Her body, her choice if not pimped |
| Resistant diseases | Stem cells based medication to cure |
| Famine | Technologies to produce fresh water |
| Nanotechnology | Peaceful and productive applications |
| Leaders | Visionaries and motivators, not rulers |
| Type A Personalities | They need to chill out for psych eval |
| Bullies | Find root causes made them that way |

Conclusion:

The present socio-economic paradigms serve to keep the system of things moving in a more or less orderly and somewhat predictable manner. However, the inherent volatility in the entire global system lies in the weaknesses dependent upon consumer confidence and choices. Changing consumer attitudes is not an easy task, but the loss of consumer confidence can and has occurred overnight in a twinkling of an eye. Exploring alternative realities enable social and economic planners to "see outside of the box" and be able to anticipate and adjust to any unforeseen changes that threaten society.

America is only as great as its people's willingness to adapt to adversity and through collective will and creativity develop better solutions that benefit the entire nation and all of its people across the socioeconomic strata from rich to poor in every state, cities and towns in the diverse and rich landscape. Both the strengths and weaknesses in America is not determined by the elites and power brokers in a vacuum, but rather, these groups usurp the power of the people because people permit it to happen primarily due to apathy, mass media indoctrination, and the belief that individuals are powerless against "the system" to effect positive changes. No wonder special interests groups are controlling the politicians. Is there hope? Perhaps if positive changes become popular, then needed popular changes will come over time.